# Montana's DAR Markers:

## Honoring Where History Was Made

By Montana State Society
Daughters of the American Revolution
State Historic Preservation Committee co-chairs, 2017-2019
Janice S. Hand and Cheryl A. Genovese

# MONTANA'S DAR MARKERS:
## HONORING WHERE HISTORY WAS MADE

Copyright © 2019 by Montana State Society Daughters of the American Revolution, Helena Montana

All rights reserved. This book may not be reproduced in any form or by electronic or mechanical means including information storage and retrieval systems without permission in writing from the authors, with the exception of short quotes for the purpose of review.

ISBN: 978-0-578-44229-7

Library of Congress Control Number: 2019901235

10 9 8 7 6 5 4 3 2

Cover photograph: Montana State Histrorical Society Research Center Photograhy Archives, no. 757-646

# Dedication

This book is a 200-page thank you to the women of Montana State Society Daughters of the American Revolution. We appreciate and remember your 125 years of service and herein ensure that your work in placing historical markers across the state is well and truly documented.

To repeat one of the best salutes to the work of Montana DAR, made by Mr. R.C. Dilavou, principal speaker at the DAR marker dedication at Pompey's Pillar:

*Ladies of the DAR, I salute you upon the great work you have accomplished in the past. I congratulate you upon the work that you are now doing. And I leave with you, full of confidence in your patriotism and loyalty, the many opportunities that lie before you during the coming years.*

Starting in 1908, Montana DAR has installed 70 historical markers across the state. Of those, 33 remain. This book records why the markers' sites were selected, their history, and the back story of each.

Today, placing historic markers seems to be an anachronism. Why bother? An answer comes from 1925, when David Hilger, state librarian of the Montana Historical Society said:

*Let the future historian ponder when he reads the inscription on this tablet, let him ponder upon the deeds of valor and sacrifice made by the men and women of that time. Let him contemplate for just a brief moment conditions then existing in a new country far from civilized communities; far from the base of supply; the comforts of home and modern surroundings; among hostile Indians; with storm and tempest, drought and dust, injury and sickness; and you have a brief story of our Montana pioneers ...*

# ABOUT DAR

The Daughters of the American Revolution is a non-profit, non-political volunteer service organization of 180,000 women dedicated to preserving American history, securing America's future through better education, and promoting patriotism. DAR's motto is *God, Home and Country*.

DAR was founded October 11, 1890, by four women who created the organization to "perpetuate the memory and spirit of the women and men who achieved American independence." Since its founding, over 950,000 women have been admitted to DAR in 3,000 chapters in the U.S. and in units overseas. Membership is open to all who are descendants of a Patriot who supported the effort for independence.

The state of Montana has ten DAR chapters. See www.montanadar.org and www.dar.org.

## TERMS

- **MSSDAR** – Montana State Society Daughters of the American Revolution
- **SAR** – Sons of the American Revolution
- **HODAR** – Husband of Daughter of the American Revolution
- **State Regent** – leads all of the chapters within the state
- **Chapter Regent** – leads the individual DAR chapter
- **Chapter** – of Montana's ten chapters, eight have historic markers nearby: Bitter Root (Missoula area), Black Eagle-Assinniboine (Great Falls area), Julia Hancock (Lewistown area), Milk River (Malta area), Mount Hyalite (Bozeman area), Oro Fino (Helena area), Shining Mountain (Billings area), Silver Bow (Butte area). The other two Montana DAR chapters are Chief Ignace (Kalispell area) and Kuilix (Mission Valley area).

This book is organized by the area in which each DAR marker is sited, in alphabetic order by nearest town. See the Montana map on page xiv.

# Table of Contents

Dedication ................................................................................................ i
Preface .................................................................................................... v
    Sponsoring DAR Chapters by Marker and Year ........................... vii
Acknowledgements ............................................................................. xi
    Finding Montana's DAR Markers ................................................. xii
    Map of Montana's DAR Markers ................................................. xiv
1. Lewis and Clark Yellowstone River Journey .................................. 1
2. World War I Memorial Trees ........................................................... 5
3. Pompey's Pillar/Captain Clark Signature ....................................... 9
4. Fort Ellis ........................................................................................... 15
5. Lindley Park .................................................................................... 19
6. Founder's House ............................................................................. 23
7. Pay Gold ........................................................................................... 27
8. Spanish-American War Veterans Memorial ................................ 33
9. Dillon's Founding ........................................................................... 37
10. Pathfinder Tribute ........................................................................ 41
11. Historic Bannack .......................................................................... 45
12. Sacajawea Memorial-Armstead ................................................. 51
13. Southern Gateway ........................................................................ 57
14. Old Fort Benton Blockhouse ...................................................... 63
15. Old Fort Peck ................................................................................ 71
16. Montana Real Daughter Orpha Zilpha Parke Bovee ............... 75
17. Giant Springs ................................................................................ 81
18. Veterans Memorial Tree .............................................................. 85
19. Fort Custer ..................................................................................... 89

20. Rosebud Battlefield ..................................................................... 93
21. Bear Paw Battlefield .................................................................... 97
22. Fort Assinniboine ..................................................................... 103
23. Gates of The Mountains ............................................................ 107
24. Reed and Bowles Stockade Trading Post .................................... 113
25. Reed's Fort Post Office .............................................................. 119
26. Teigen School ........................................................................... 125
27. First Lewis and Clark Trail Marker ............................................ 129
28. Travelers' Rest .......................................................................... 133
29. Boot Hill Cemetery ................................................................... 139
30. Fort Keogh Officer Quarters ..................................................... 143
31. Montana Real Daughter Caroline Reed Stone ........................... 147
32. Sacajawea Memorial-Three Forks .............................................. 153
33. Fort Logan Blockhouse ............................................................. 159
34. Lost DAR Markers ................................................................... 165
    Beaverhead Rock ......................................................................... 165
    Camp Fortunate .......................................................................... 171
    Lewis and Clark Trail Markers through Beaverhead County ...... 174
    Lewis and Clark Trail Markers - Bear Island to Grand Falls ...... 178
    Madison River Toll Bridge and Tipi Rings ................................. 178
35. Other DAR Commemorations ................................................. 181
    Montana Copper Spade ............................................................. 181
    The Washington Elm .................................................................. 185
    Sacajawea Recreation Area, Lemhi Pass ..................................... 187
    George Washington Bicentennial DAR Tree .............................. 191
    First State Regent ....................................................................... 192
    DAR-SAR 125th Anniversary Tree ............................................. 195

# Preface

At Montana State DAR's 21st state conference in 1924, DAR decided that "a definite program should be carried out crystalizing in the placing of a bronze marker or two each year, until at least the most noteworthy landmarks, and sites, in the state had been thus designated." Among the chairs of the committee over the years were Laura Tolman Scott (Beaverhead Chapter), Mrs. C.A. Rasmusson (Oro Fino Chapter), and Mrs. E. Broox Martin (Mount Hyalite Chapter).

The Markers Committee developed a Bronze Marker Program for placing 25 bronze tablets, two each year, on historic sites designated by the Committee for Marking of Historic Spots and Old Trails, chaired by Laura Tolman Scott. As Mrs. Rasmusson related:

> *This was made possible through the magnificent generosity of…the Anaconda Copper Mining Company.… It is a source of great state pride to know that these tablets are made of native Montana copper and related ores, and are fashioned in a Montana foundry by the ingenuity and handiwork of Montana men. Each of these markers is 24 by 36 inches in size, weighs 165 pounds, carries an appropriate inscription, with the DAR insignia in the lower left-hand corner.*

The largest proportion of bronze markers was donated by the Anaconda Copper Mining Company (ACM). Of the original 18 that ACM donated to DAR, 17 remain to this day and can be found at these sites:

1. Bear Paw Battlefield
2. Fort Assinniboine
3. Fort Custer
4. Fort Ellis

5. Fort Logan *(believed to be ACM tablet, but unconfirmed)*
6. Gates of the Mountains
7. Giant Springs
8. Historic Bannack
9. Pathfinder Tribute
10. Pay Gold
11. Pompey's Pillar/Captain Clark Signature
12. Reed and Bowles Stockade Trading Post
13. Reed's Fort Post Office
14. Rosebud Battlefield
15. Sacajawea Memorial-Armstead
16. Southern Gateway
17. Travelers' Rest
18. *(Beaverhead Rock-lost)*

## DAR Marker Sites at State Parks

1. Bannack State Park, Bannack
2. Giant Springs State Park, Great Falls
3. Rosebud Battlefield State Park, Hardin
4. Travelers' Rest State Park, Lolo
5. *Beaverhead Rock State Park, Dillon (marker lost)*
6. *Clark's Lookout State Park, Dillon (marker lost)*

# Sponsoring DAR Chapters by Marker and Year

Almost all Montana DAR chapters have placed historic markers in their communities, starting in 1908 and continuing through 2019. The next two tables show markers by sponsoring chapter and by the date they were originally installed.

TABLE I – SPONSORING DAR CHAPTERS

| Installing Chapter | Markers (in date order) |
|---|---|
| **Beaverhead** (now Silver Bow) | Pathfinder Tribute, Dillon's Founding, Southern Gateway |
| | *Lost: Beaverhead Rock, Camp Fortunate, Lewis and Clark Trail Markers Through Beaverhead County* |
| | *Other Commemorations: Sacajawea Recreation Area-Lemhi Pass* |
| **Bitter Root** | Travelers' Rest |
| **Black Eagle-Assinniboine** | Giant Springs, Fort Assinniboine, Veterans Memorial Tree, Montana Real Daughter Caroline Reed Stone |
| | *Lost: Lewis and Clark Trail Markers Between Bear Island and Grand Falls* |
| **Julia Hancock** | Reed's Fort Post Office, Reed and Bowles Stockade Trading Post, Teigen School |
| **Milk River** | Fort Peck |
| **Mount Hyalite** | First Lewis and Clark Trail Marker, Lindley Park, Fort Ellis |
| | *Lost: Madison River Toll Bridge and Tipi Rings* |
| **Oro Fino** | Fort Logan Blockhouse, Gates of the Mountains |
| | *Lost: The Washington Elm* |

| | |
|---|---|
| **Powder River** (now Shining Mountain) | Fort Keogh Officer Quarters, Boot Hill Cemetery |
| **Shining Mountain** | Lewis and Clark Yellowstone River Journey, World War I Memorial Trees, Pompey's Pillar/Captain Clark Signature, Fort Custer, Rosebud Battlefield |
| | *Lost: George Washington Bicentennial DAR Tree* |
| **Silver Bow** | Spanish-American War Veterans Memorial, Pay Gold, Founder's House |
| **Montana State Society DAR** | Sacajawea Memorial-Three Forks, Sacajawea Memorial-Armstead, Historic Bannack, Bear Paw Battlefield, Montana Real Daughter Orpha Zilpha Parke Bovee, Old Fort Benton Blockhouse |
| | *Other Commemorations: Montana Copper Spade, First State Regent, 125$^{th}$ Anniversary DAR-SAR Tree* |

TABLE II – MARKERS BY YEAR INITIALLY PLACED

| Year | Marker |
|---|---|
| 1902 | *Montana Copper Spade-other commemoration* |
| 1908 | Spanish-American War Veterans Memorial, First Lewis and Clark Trail Marker |
| 1914 | Sacajawea Memorial-Three Forks |
| 1915 | Sacajawea Memorial-Armstead |
| 1921 | *Numerous small metal signs in Beaverhead County-lost* |
| 1922 | *Six small metal signs in Beaverhead County-lost* |
| 1923 | Lindley Park, *two small metal signs in Beaverhead County (Boiling Springs, Jackson)-lost* |
| 1924 | Fort Logan Blockhouse, Lewis and Clark Yellowstone River Journey, *nine small metal signs at Bannack-lost* |
| 1925 | Historic Bannack, Travelers' Rest |
| 1926 | Fort Ellis, *small metal sign at Three Thousand Mile Island-lost* |
| 1927 | Gates of the Mountains, WWI Memorial Trees, *Clark's Lookout-lost* |
| 1928 | Giant Springs, Pathfinder Tribute, Pompey's Pillar/Captain Clark Signature |
| 1929 | Bear Paw Battlefield |
| 1930 | Dillon's Founding, Fort Custer |
| 1931 | Pay Gold, Reed's Fort Post Office |
| 1932 | *The Washington Elm, Sacajawea Recreation Area-Lemhi Pass, George Washington Bicentennial DAR ree-other commemorations* |
| 1934 | Rosebud Battlefield |
| 1935 | Southern Gateway |
| 1937 | *Camp Fortunate-lost* |
| 1940 | Reed and Bowles Stockade Trading Post |
| 1947 | Montana Real Daughter Orpha Zilpha Parke Bovee |
| 1955 | *Beaverhead Rock-lost* |
| 1958 | Fort Assinniboine |

| | |
|---|---|
| **1964** | *Madison River Toll Bridge and Tipi Rings-lost* |
| **1970** | Fort Peck |
| **1976** | Boot Hill Cemetery, Fort Keogh Officer Quarters, Teigen School |
| **1977** | *First State Regent-other commemoration* |
| **2006** | Founder's House, Veterans Memorial Tree |
| **2010** | Montana Real Daughter Caroline Reed Stone |
| **2019** | 125th Anniversary DAR-SAR Tree, Old Fort Benton Blockhouse |

---

*May our past record inspire us to reconsecrate our efforts and to do more and more. We are living in the period of Montana's development when we are becoming conscious that we have a history. A history made up of enchanting tales more fascinating than fiction, and landmarks holding far greater glamour than the older shrines of the east.*

There's nothing that the public so appreciates as signs pointing to noted spots. Stranger tourists flock to well-marked places. The locality in itself may be barren and mean and commonplace, but nothing so quickens the imagination as to be actually on the spot where famous events took place; to look with one's own eyes on the places rendered interesting by our heroes and the deeds that make us love and honor them.

We seem to have walked and talked and rejoiced and sorrowed with them; to have made friends with them in their old homes and haunts.

(By Laura Tolman Scott, chair of the Montana DAR Committee on Preservation of Historic Spots, 1929)

# ACKNOWLEDGEMENTS

This book has been 125 years in the making. It stands on the shoulders of prior authors and all who love Montana history. With appreciation to:

**Earlier DAR authors** who kept our marker information alive (esp. Mrs. C.A. Rasmusson, Mrs. Fred E. May, Iris McKinney Gray, Mrs. R.V. Love, Mrs. E.E. Bruno, Mrs. Sidney Groff and Miss E. Lorene Burks);

**Cameo Society** for its enthusiastic support and financial backing;

**State Regent Jane Lee Hamman** for being a champion of the book, for sharing historic facts, and for her always helpful edits;

**Montana DAR chapters** whose members went out to take photographs and get GPS coordinates (esp. the chapter regent who took unsuspecting out of town guests on a "DAR marker treasure hunt");

**Sandy Taylor** (Chief Ignace Chapter) for typing the initial book draft from dim photocopies and for her eyestrain while proofreading the book;

**Char Ross** (Black Eagle-Assinniboine Chapter), along with John, her HODAR and SAR member, who traveled 520 miles on their 2010 Harley Davidson motorcycle recording DAR markers, who researched historic facts, and who dug out a potential marker from two feet of February snow;

**Jennifer Buckley** (Silver Bow Chapter) for deep digging through dozens of old newspapers to ensure that our facts are correct, and to her HODAR, Luke, for the GPS map;

**Rick Sanders** (Janice S. Hand's HODAR) for suffering endless hours providing help with malevolent software and for cover design; and

The **State Historical Society** for research assistance and permission from its Research Center Photography Archives to print its historic photos.

# Finding Montana's DAR Markers

| In or near: | Monument (with book chapter number) |
|---|---|
| Billings | 1. Lewis and Clark Yellowstone River Journey |
| Billings | 2. WW I Memorial Trees |
| Billings | 3. Pompey's Pillar/Captain Clark Signature |
| Bozeman | 4. Fort Ellis |
| Bozeman | 5. Lindley Park |
| Butte | 6. Founder's House |
| Butte | 7. Pay Gold |
| Butte | 8. Spanish-American War Veterans Memorial |
| Dillon | 9. Dillon's Founding |
| Dillon | 10. Pathfinder Tribute |
| Dillon | 11. Historic Bannack |
| Dillon | 12. Sacajawea Marker-Armstead |
| Dillon | 13. Southern Gateway |
| Fort Benton | 14. Old Fort Benton Blockhouse |
| Glasgow | 15. Old Fort Peck |
| Glendive | 16. Mont. Real Daughter Orpha Z.P. Bovee |
| Great Falls | 17. Giant Springs |
| Great Falls | 18. Veterans Memorial Tree |
| Hardin | 19. Fort Custer |
| Hardin | 20. Rosebud Battlefield |
| Havre | 21. Bear Paw Battlefield |
| Havre | 22. Fort Assinniboine |
| Helena | 23. Gates of the Mountains |
| Lewistown | 24. Reed and Bowles Stockade Trading Post |
| Lewistown | 25. Reed's Fort Post Office |
| Lewistown | 26. Teigen School |

| | | |
|---|---|---|
| Livingston | 27. | First Lewis and Clark Trail Marker |
| Lolo | 28. | Travelers' Rest |
| Miles City | 29. | Boot Hill Cemetery |
| Miles City | 30. | Fort Keogh Officer Quarters |
| Shelby | 31. | Mont. Real Daughter Caroline Reed Stone |
| Three Forks | 32. | Sacajawea Memorial-Three Forks |
| White Sulphur Springs | 33. | Fort Logan Block House |

---

*From* **The Dillon Examiner** *newspaper, April 3, 1929, "State D.A.R. Endeavors to Mark and Perpetuate"*

*We are living in the period of Montana's development when we are becoming conscious that we have a history. A history made up of enchanting tales more fascinating than fiction, and landmarks holding far greater glamour than the older shrines of the east.*

*The Daughters have been entrusted with a precious heritage: that of reviving and perpetuating the memory and spirit of these scenes. The work of each Historic Spots Committee this year is threefold. First, to locate, preserve, and mark places of historic importance; second, to conduct the "most historic" contest; and third, to collect the material for the "National Road Guide."*

(By Laura Tolman Scott, chair of the Montana DAR Committee on Preservation of Historic Spots)

# Map of Montana's DAR Markers

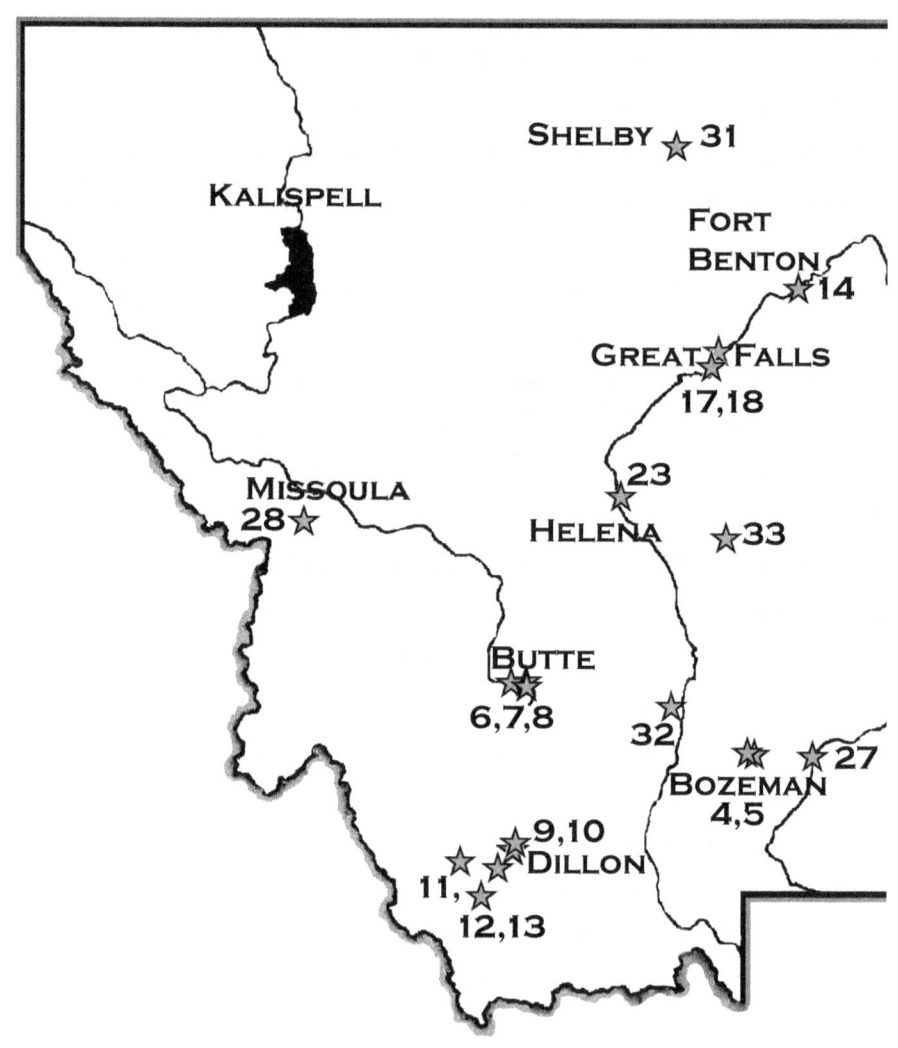

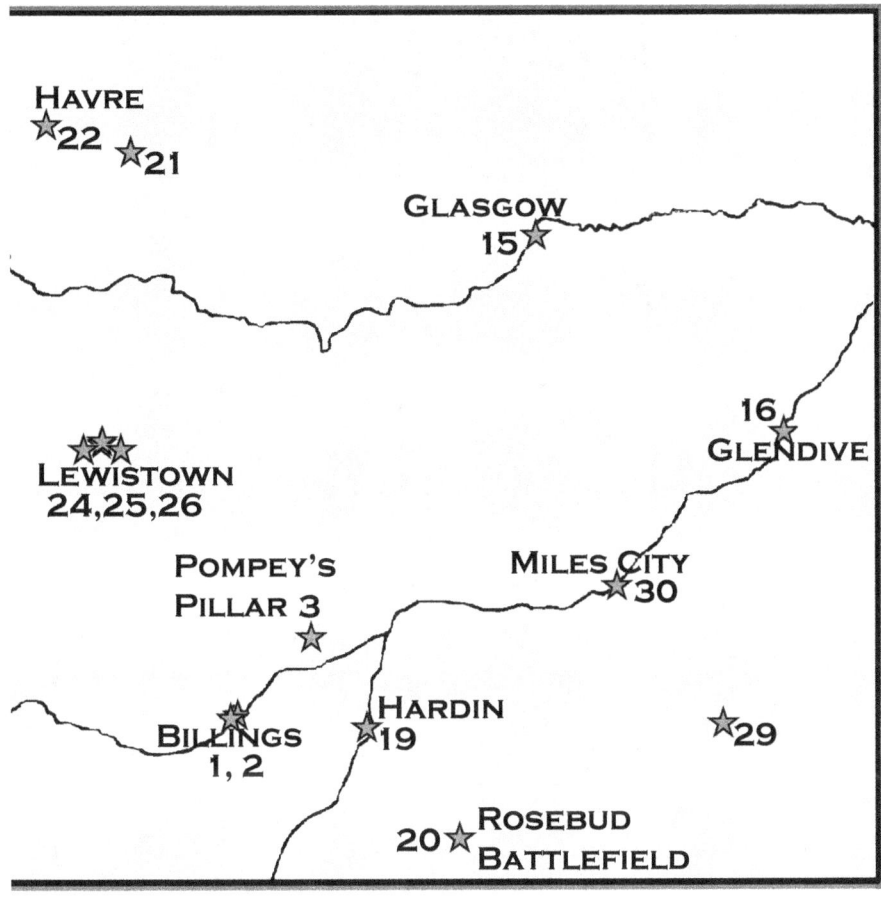

# MONTANA

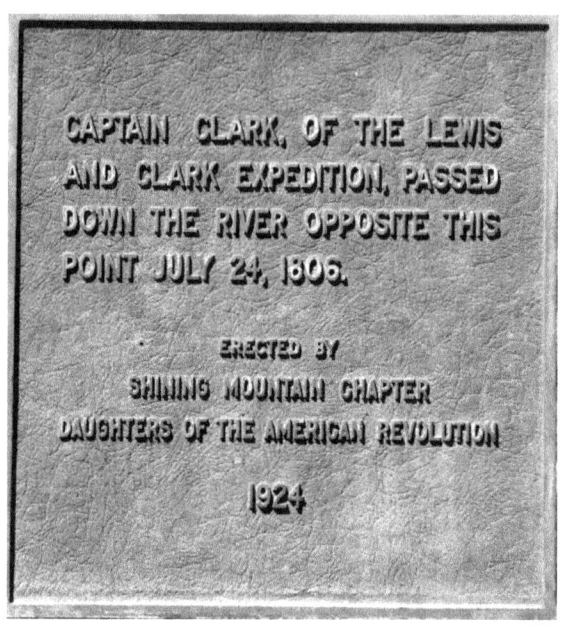

*Lewis and Clark Yellowstone River Journey marker (above) and site location (below), 2017*

# 1. LEWIS AND CLARK YELLOWSTONE RIVER JOURNEY

Billings
GPS coordinates: 45.800124 | -108.478056

| | |
|---|---|
| **Commemorates** | The point on the Yellowstone River where Captain Clark of the Lewis and Clark Expedition passed down the river on July 24, 1806 |
| **Site Location** | *Original*: Midland Empire Fairgrounds, Billings *Replacement*: In Billings MetraPark Arena (Yellowstone County Fairgrounds), right of the Montana Pro Rodeo Wall of Fame |
| **Installed** | *Original:* October 7, 1924 |
| | *Replaced:* October 8, 1979 |
| **Wording** | "Captain Clark, of the Lewis and Clark Expedition, passed down the river opposite this point July 24, 1806. Erected by Shining Mountain Chapter Daughters of the American Revolution, 1924" *(original and replacement markers are identical)* |

# History

This marker was erected October 7, 1924, to commemorate the journey of Lewis and Clark down the Yellowstone River at a point which they passed near present day Billings on July 24, 1806, on their return trip from the Pacific Coast. It was a three-foot square bronze marker placed on a granite rock at the Midland Empire Fair Grounds in Billings. The first of Shining Mountain Chapter, NSDAR's historic markers, it was dedicated during the 21$^{st}$ Montana DAR State Conference in Billings. It was at that conference where, for the first time, Montana hosted two national officers, President General Mrs. Anthony W. Cooke and Organizing Secretary General Mrs. William S. Walker. The national president general assisted in presenting the marker.

In 1969, a fire destroyed the Midland Empire Fair Exposition Hall and melted the original DAR bronze tablet. The Yellowstone Metra, which replaced the former fairground building, was built in the 1970s.

On October 8, 1979, the Shining Mountain Chapter DAR presented a duplicate of the original plaque placed in another boulder near the west doors of the new fairgrounds building. During the ceremony, Metra manager Robert Glasgow, Yellowstone County Commission Chair Mike McClintock, and Billings Mayor William Fox accepted the marker on behalf of all who attend events at the venue. Three Montana State DAR officers took part in the ceremony–State Regent Mrs. Orrion Pilon of Dillon, State Vice Regent Mrs. Frank Pickett of Bozeman, and State Chaplain Mrs. Ervin Becker of Billings. Chapter Regent Mrs. Garrett Cornelius was mistress of ceremonies.

SOURCES

- Historic monument records, Office of the Historian General, Washington D.C.
- *Record of Tablets and Markers Placed by Montana DAR 1908-1947*, by Mrs. Fred E. May
- *State Centennial History, MSSDAR*, by Iris McKinney Gray, Vol. V 1894-1994
- *Historical Sites Preserved and Markers Erected by MSSDAR and Its Chapters, 1899-1977*, by Mrs. R.V. Love and Mrs. E.E. Bruno
- *MSSDAR 1982-1984 Pictorial Supplement to Historic Events of 1894-1977*, by Mrs. R.V. Love, Mrs. Sidney Groff and Miss Lorene Burks
- *Daughters of the American Revolution Magazine* archives, Vol. 58, No. 12, December 1924, pg. 772
- *Daughters of the American Revolution Magazine* archives, Vol. 114, No. 2, February 1980, pg. 185
- *Billings Gazette* newspaper, Billings Montana, "Marker Unveiled," Oct. 8, 1924, pg. 1

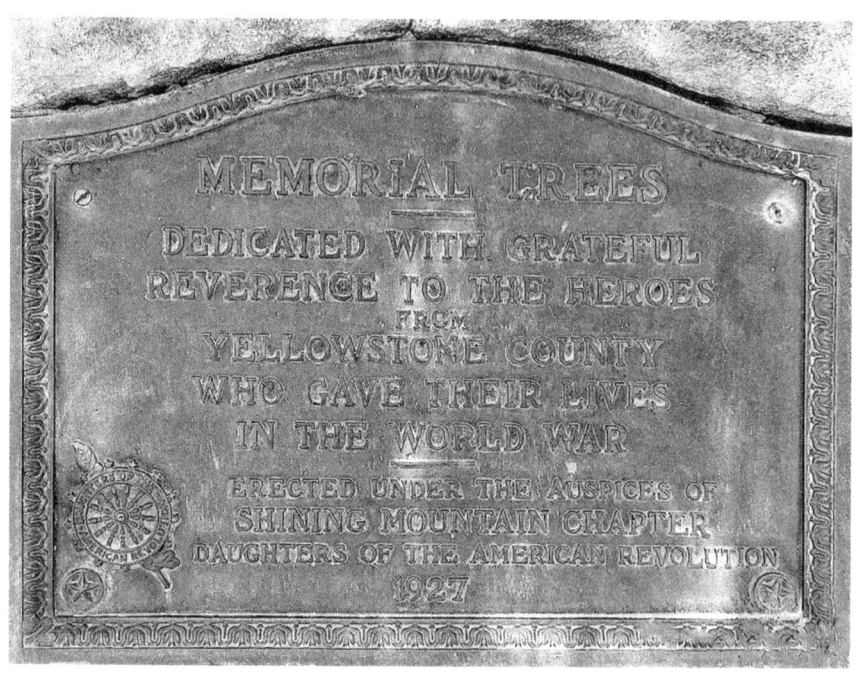

*World War I Memorial Trees marker (above), "doghouse" (below), 2017*

# 2. World War I Memorial Trees

Billings
GPS coordinates of original: 45.78406 | -108.525255
GPS coordinates at rededication: 45.784084 | -108.525261

| | |
|---|---|
| **Commemorates** | Honoring soldiers and a nurse who lost their lives in World War I |
| **Site Location** | *Original*: east side of Senior High School in Billings |
| **Installed** | *Original*: May 19, 1927 |
| | Rededicated: May 1986 |
| **Wording** | *Original*: "Memorial Trees. Dedicated with grateful reverence to the heroes from Yellowstone County who gave their lives in the World War. Erected under the auspices of Shining Mountain Chapter Daughters of the American Revolution May 19, 1927" |
| | *Rededicated*: "Shining Mountain Chapter Daughters of the American Revolution 1927 – Rededicated – 1986" |

# History

Memorial Drive was dedicated May 19, 1927, to honor 52 soldiers and a nurse from Yellowstone County who sacrificed their lives in World War I. The Shining Mountain Chapter, NSDAR and various Billings patriotic and service clubs gathered at Pioneer Park for the ceremony. The DAR plaque was installed on the right hand pier of a stone gateway built at the Grand Avenue entrance. The gateway wall was built by Mr. A. Jacobucci. Originally, an elm tree was planted for each individual, and at the base of each was a sloping concrete block 10 inches square, into which was embedded a bronze disc decorated with laurel leaves and inscribed with the full name and death of each soldier and the nurse. DAR member Mrs. F.W. Adams, who was responsible for the original idea of the Avenue of Memorial Trees, chaired the chapter's memorial committee working with Mrs. A.J. McIntyre, Mrs. J.G. Sherman, Mrs. Frank Woods, and Mrs. Harry Allen.

After the Billings Boy's Band played the "Star-Spangled Banner," the occasion was made solemn by the requiem "Taps." Reverend Weaver, a Sons of the American Revolution member, delivered the invocation. Chapter Regent Mrs. H.E. Reckard and Vice Regent Gertrude Crippen unveiled the boulder and presented the memorial to the city. Mrs. Reckard said, "We have used the tree as a living symbol that the influence of their deeds will grow and spread as the branches flourish."

The lane of trees was located on the east side of Senior High School in Billings. Unfortunately, Dutch elm disease wiped out the trees. The individual markers were removed and stored and there has not yet been found a suitable permanent home for them.

At the entrance to the drive is a bronze tablet embedded in stone. Close-by, also located near the bronze tablet, is a small structure with a red marble rooftop. The top is inscribed with the names of those honored by the bronze markers originally placed at the foot of each memorial tree. A granite plaque was placed on the small structure during the 1986 rededication. It reads: "Shining Mountain Chapter Daughters of the American Revolution 1927 – Rededicated – 1986." The chapter raised $3,000 for the monument.

SOURCES
- Historic monument records, Office of the Historian General, Washington D.C.
- *Record of Tablets and Markers Placed by Montana DAR 1908-1947*, by Mrs. Fred E. May
- *State Centennial History, MSSDAR*, by Iris McKinney Gray, Vol. V 1894-1994
- *Historical Sites Preserved and Markers Erected by MSSDAR and Its Chapters 1899-1977*, by Mrs. R.V. Love and Mrs. E.E. Bruno
- *MSSDAR 1982-1984 Pictorial Supplement to Historic Events of 1894-1977*, by Mrs. R.V. Love, Mrs. Sidney Groff and Miss Lorene Burks
- *DAR American Revolution Magazine* archives, August 1928, pps. 494-495
- *The Billings Gazette* newspaper, "Memorial Monument," May 27, 1986, pg. 12

*Pompey's Pillar/Captain Clark Signature marker (above) and site (top, largest) with Captain Clark's signature under glass (lower right)*

# 3. Pompey's Pillar/Captain Clark Signature

25 miles east of Billings
GPS coordinates: 45.995473 | -108.004760

| | |
|---|---|
| **Commemorates** | Site's discovery and naming by Captain Clark of the Lewis and Clark Expedition, which includes his inscribed signature, believed to be the only such left by the Expedition |
| **Site Location** | Pompey's Pillar National Monument and National Historic Landmark, off of I-94 |
| **Installed** | May 24, 1928 |
| **Wording** | "Pompey's Pillar. Discovered and named by Captain William Clark of the Lewis and Clark Expedition July 25, 1806. With Clark returning down the Yellowstone were: Pryor, Shannon, Bratton, Windsor, Hall, Shields, Gibson, Labiche, Chaboneau, Sacajawea and child, York the slave. In gratitude to Lewis and Clark, those intrepid leaders, to Sacajawea, their unerring guide, and to the Fidelity and Courage of all the company. This tablet is dedicated by Shining Mountain Chapter Daughters of the American Revolution, Billings, Montana May 24, 1928" |

# History

First named by Captain William A. Clark as "Pompey's Tower," Pompey's Pillar is a huge sandstone formation rising 150 feet above the Yellowstone River that was discovered by Clark on his return from the Pacific Northwest on his journey down the Yellowstone River. The pillar is a sandstone history book that reads like a who's who of western frontier history. The rock face shows the remains of animal drawings created by people who used the area for rendezvous, campsites, and hunting over 11,000 years.

Naming the anomalous natural formation after Sacajawea's child Jean Baptiste Charbonneau or 'Pomp,' Clark wrote of the discovery in his journal that evening:

> ... at 4PM [I] arrived at the remarkable rock situated in an extensive bottom. This rock I ascended and from it's top had a most extensive view in every direction. This rock which I shall call Pompy's Tower is 200 feet high and 400 paces in secumpherance and only axcessible on one side which is from the N.E. the other parts of it being a perpendicular clift of lightish coloured gritty rock. The Indians have made 2 piles of stone on the top of this tower... [sic] (Jones 2000, 185-186)

During his stay there, Captain Clark carved his signature into the face of the rock. It reads: "Wm Clark, July 25, 1806." The Northern Pacific Railway was completed in 1882 and provided transportation through the Yellowstone River Valley. Passengers stopping at the Northern Pacific Railway station a half-mile south of the Pillar routinely visited the Pillar to view Clark's inscription. Over the years, the letters began to fade and were vulnerable to both further erosion as well as vandals.

In 1882, the Northern Pacific Railway decided to protect Clark's signature by covering it with a heavy iron screen. In 1926, at the urging of Shining Mountain Chapter, NSDAR, Northern Pacific Railway district freight and passenger agent J.E. Spurling received authorization from the company to hire Hazelton Brothers of Billings Marble and Granite Works to cut the signature deeper. As a result, a local paper reported, "The deepening of the letters has restored the inscription to its original state and it can now be easily read from the railroad tracks."

On May 24, 1928, 20 DAR members dedicated a large bronze plaque installed on Pompey's Pillar's perpendicular face in front of an audience of 130. (It was the second historic marker installed by this chapter.) The large bronze plaque was donated by the Anaconda Copper Mining Company. The husband of Shining Mountain Chapter DAR's regent, R.C. Dilavou, gave the keynote speech. In remarks, he noted: "Many of us have been inclined to think that the historic spots of our nation are all in the eastern, or New England states, but much of the history of our country has been made in the west as well."

In Regent Mrs. R.C. Dilavou's dedicatory address, she said,

*Today we stand on a hallowed spot which 122 years ago was but a camping ground in a high adventure. As we look up and down a peaceful and productive valley filled with the homes of American citizens, with schools, churches, and thriving business enterprises, it is difficult for us to reconstruct the scene upon which Capt. William Clark and his followers gazed that July day nearly a century and a quarter ago....We cannot but wonder if that intrepid soldier and explorer grasped even a hint of what his journey was to mean eventually to this great northwest.*

In 1968, Don C. Foote, the then-owner of Pompey's Pillar, moved the DAR plaque to a spot close to the Captain Clark signature.

*(**Note 1**: Clark likely playfully dedicated and autographed the Pillar for Sacajawea's young son, Baptiste, of whom the Captain was very fond. Pompey or "Bampe" is the Shoshone word for head and one of Sacajawea's pet names for her baby was Pompey–he was her first or "head" child. A landmark had been named for just about everyone else in the party. In Clark's eyes, the rock rose up like a huge head, hence the name "Pompey's Tower," which later became Pompey's Pillar.)*

*(**Note 2**: Sacajawea's husband's name is shown in historic records spelled two ways–Chaboneau and later, Charbonneau. The 1928 marker uses the older spelling.)*

SOURCES

- Historic monument records, Office of the Historian General, Washington D.C.
- *Record of Tablets and Markers Placed by Montana DAR 1908-1947*, by Mrs. Fred E. May
- *State Centennial History, MSSDAR,* by Iris McKinney Gray, Vol. V 1894-1994
- *Historical Sites Preserved and Markers Erected by MSSDAR and Its Chapters 1899-1977*, by Mrs. R.V. Love and Mrs. E.E. Bruno
- *MSSDAR 1982-1984 Pictorial Supplement to Historic Events of 1894-1977*, by Mrs. R.V. Love, Mrs. Sidney Groff and Miss Lorene Burks
- "Lewis and Clark Expedition: Pompey's Pillar," by National Park Service, at https://www.nps.gov/nr/travel/lewisand Clark/pom.htm
- *The Billings Gazette* newspaper, Billings Montana, "Pompeys Pillar Mark Restored," Oct. 13, 1926, pg. 7
- *The Billings Gazette* newspaper, Billings Montana, "Pompey Tablet to be Unveiled," May 24, 1928, pg. 11
- *The Billings Gazette newspaper*, Billings Montana, "Pompeys Piller Is Marked With Tablet," May 25, 1928, pg. 9
- *The Billings Gazette newspaper*, Billings Montana, "Pillar Plaque Moved to Different Place," June 28, 1968

*May 25, 1928, Billings Gazette newspaper*

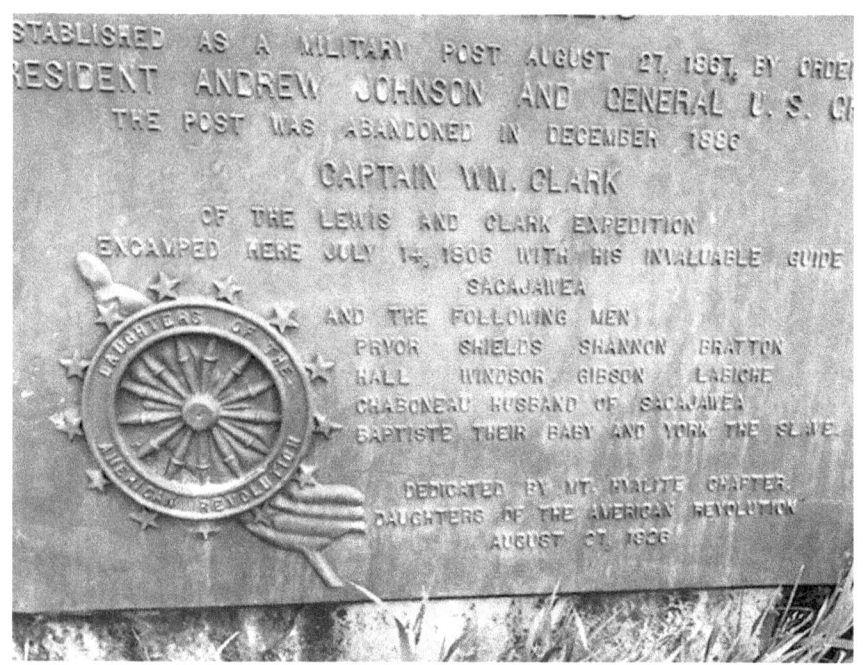

*Fort Ellis DAR marker (above) and site of marker (below), 2017*

# 4. FORT ELLIS

Near Bozeman
GPS coordinates: 45.66854229 | -110.9753965

| | |
|---|---|
| **Commemorates** | The last abandoned frontier fort and campsite of Captain William Clark and company |
| **Site Location** | One mile east of Bozeman |
| **Installed** | August 27, 1926 |
| **Wording** | "Fort Ellis established as a military post August 27, 1867 by order of President Andrew Johnson and General U.S. Grant. The post was abandoned in December 1886. Captain Wm. Clark of the Lewis and Clark Expedition camped here July 14, 1806 with his invaluable Sacajawea and the following men: Pryor, Shields, Shannon, Bratton, Hall, Windsor, Gibson, Labiche, Charbonneau husband of Sacajawea, Baptiste their baby, and York the slave. Dedicated by Mt. Hyalite Chapter Daughters of the American Revolution August 27, 1926." |

# History

On August 27, 1926, in evening ceremonies, the Mount Hyalite Chapter, NSDAR placed a native copper tablet on a boulder at the site of old Fort Ellis at an event attended by over 500 people. The monument, surrounded by a wreath of sweet pea flowers, was erected a few feet from where the fort's sundial stood. Chapter Regent Mrs. M.P. Davidson presided, and Mrs. C.A. Rasmusson of Helena, chair of the DAR Historic Preservation Committee gave the dedicatory address, expressing appreciation to the Anaconda Copper Mining Company for the gift of the tablet. Mrs. Rasmusson's remarks included:

> *The simple legends on signs like this one at Fort Ellis will raise up a treasury of golden texts for impressive sermons on patriotism, and now, on behalf of the National Society of the Daughters of the American Revolution, it becomes my privilege to dedicate this memorial to the memory of the brave men who were stationed here and who served their country well. We entrust its protection to you people of the Gallatin valley, your children, and generations to come.*

Mrs. E. Broox Martin of Bozeman, a member of the state DAR Marker Committee, made the presentation to Gallatin County. The American flags draping the monument were then drawn by Robert McKee and Oliver Whitcomb, children of DAR members.

Fort Ellis was established as a U.S. Army post on August 27, 1867 at the recommendation of General H. Terry, then commanding the Department of Dakota (Dakota Territory). The fort was approved by General Ulysses S. Grant, Commander of the Armies of the United States, and the executive order for its establishment was signed by President Andrew Johnson. It was named in honor of Colonel

Augustus Van Horn Ellis of the 124th New York Volunteers, who was killed in 1863 at the Battle of Gettysburg during the Civil War. The fort was built by Captain R.S. LaMotte and three companies of the 13th Infantry to protect miners and settlers moving in the Gallatin Valley.

Later that year, General Gibbons started his column from Fort Ellis to join General H. Terry in the expedition to the Battle of the Little Big Horn. Fort Ellis Captain James Bradley, an intrepid soldier and accomplished writer, was the first to discover the bodies of General George Armstrong Custer and his troops on the fatal battlefield. It was from Fort Ellis that a detachment was sent to join the fight at the Bear Paw Mountains with Chief Joseph. There Captain Bradley lost his life.

Fort Ellis, one of the last of the old Northwest frontier forts to be abandoned, was closed by the U.S. government in December 1886.

Earlier in the 19th century on July 14, 1806, Captain William Clark had camped near the later fort site on the return of his Expedition, and on the summit of what is known as Bozeman Pass, Sacajawea had pointed out to Clark the route to the headwaters of the Yellowstone.

SOURCES
- Historic monument records, Office of the Historian General, Wash. D.C.
- *Record of Tablets and Markers Placed by Montana DAR 1908-1947*, by Mrs. Fred E. May
- *State Centennial History, MSSDAR*, by Iris McKinney Gray, 1894-1994
- *Historical Sites Preserved and Markers Erected by MSSDAR and Its Chapters 1899-1977*, by Mrs. R.V. Love and Mrs. E.E. Bruno
- *MSSDAR 1982-1984 Pictorial Supplement to Historic Events of 1894-1977*, by Mrs. R.V. Love, Mrs. Sidney Groff and Miss Lorene Burks
- *The Dillon Examiner* newspaper, Dillon Montana, "Site of Old Fort Ellis Marked by Montana D.A.R.: a Tablet of State's Native Copper," Sept. 15, 1926
- *The Billings Weekly Gazette* newspaper, Billings Montana, "D.A.R. Will Unveil Fort Ellis Marker Week From Friday," Aug. 17, 1926, pg. 3
- *The Anaconda Standard* newspaper, Anaconda Montana, "In Memory of Old Fort Ellis," Sept. 5, 1926, pg. 29

*Lindley Park DAR marker (above) and site (below), 2018*

# 5. Lindley Park

Bozeman

GPS coordinates: 45.67907865 | -111.0244

| | |
|---|---|
| **Commemorates** | The trail of the Lewis and Clark Expedition in 1805 |
| **Site Location** | Southeast entrance of Lindley Park and Sunset Hills Cemetery on East Main Street |
| **Installed** | October 26, 1923 |
| **Wording** | "This boulder marks the Trail of the Lewis and Clark Expedition 1805. Erected by the Mt. Hyalite Chapter Daughters of the American Revolution 1923" |

## History

On October 26, 1923, the Mount Hyalite Chapter, NSDAR placed the first of its historic markers on a knoll at the entrance of Lindley Park on a corner facing Main Street and leading to the Sunset Hills Cemetery. The bronze marker was set on a four-ton boulder on a cement base. Its location was chosen to be near the old trail over Cemetery Hill where Captain Clark and his party passed accompanied by the Indian woman guide Sacajawea.

According to newspapers of the day,

*When the spot was selected some time ago, the special committee from the DAR talked the matter over with the county commissioners of Gallatin County, who promised to cooperate in the movement, and said that if the women would select the boulder they would bring it down from the mountains. The committee went up West Gallatin canyon and decided upon a suitable stone, not realizing the size because it was partly underground, but the commissioners had it brought down on the county truck, and with the help of J.D. Neely and other men, under the direction of the members of the Mount Hyalite chapter DAR, they placed it on the cement base that had been prepared by the local women. The boulder weighted four tons.*

The dedication ceremony includes speeches by State Regent Mrs. E. Broox Martin, Mount Hyalite Chapter Regent Mrs. W.T. Thompson, and Jean Hamilton of Montana State College (now Montana State University). Miss Leone Lynn and Miss Jean Thompson led the flag salute and conducted the unveiling.

SOURCES

- Historic monument records, Office of the Historian General, Washington D.C.
- *Record of Tablets and Markers Placed by Montana DAR 1908-1947*, by Mrs. Fred E. May
- *State Centennial History, MSSDAR,* by Iris McKinney Gray, Vol. V 1894-1994
- *Historical Sites Preserved and Markers Erected by MSSDAR and Its Chapters 1899-1977,* by Mrs. R.V. Love and Mrs. E.E. Bruno
- *MSSDAR 1982-1984 Pictorial Supplement to Historic Events of 1894-1977,* by Mrs. R.V. Love, Mrs. Sidney Groff and Miss Lorene Burks
- *The Anaconda Standard* newspaper, Anaconda Montana, "D.A.R. to Mark Historic Spots," Aug. 9, 1923
- *The Butte Miner* newspaper, Butte Montana, "Lewis and Clark Stone Unveiled at Bozeman," Oct. 26, 1923

*Can you identify this DAR marker ceremony? (It is not the Lindley Park marker.)
Photo: Fern's Fotos by Martin (unknown date)*

*Founder's House marker (above) and the house (below), 2018*

# 6. Founder's House

Butte
GPS coordinates: 46.01225776 | -112.54869785

| | |
|---|---|
| **Commemorates** | Home of Jennie Stilwell Tallant, a founding member of Montana DAR and the first chapter regent in the state, later third state regent 1901; the site also hosted the first Montana State Society DAR state conference December 17, 1904 |
| **Site Location** | 832 West Park Street, Butte; a National Register of Historic Places site |
| **Installed** | October 21, 2006 |
| **Wording** | "Jennie Tallant, a founding member of the Montana Society Daughters of the American Revolution, and her husband Walter were early residents of this home. Named first regent of the Silver Bow DAR chapter in 1897, Jennie became the third state regent in 1901. This home was the site of many DAR meetings, including the State Society's first meeting on December 17, 1904. For that occasion, Mrs. Tallant decorated the home 'in flags and the national colors with a profusion of flowers.' |
| | Nationally, the DAR was founded in 1890 |

out of a concern that immigration was diluting American values. The society worked to promote patriotism, education, and an appreciation of American history. Among other projects, the State Society spearheaded recognition of historic sites.

Important for its DAR connection, this home, built between 1890 and 1898, is also architecturally significant. Its irregular shape, leaded glass, ornate transoms, and ornamental iron fence associate it with the popular Queen Anne style. The classical style front porch was added after 1916. In 1928, painter John Redman and his wife Mary purchased the home, which remains in the Redman family."

# History

Just one year after the National Society DAR was founded in Washington D.C. (on October 11, 1890), the National Society amended its constitution to provide for one state regent per state. It was three years after that, in 1894, that Montana received its first appointed regent, Mrs. Edmund (Mary DeVeny) Wasson, who was instructed to organize a state DAR organization. *(See the "Other DAR Commemorations" chapter.)*

Although she began her assignment, personal family tragedy interfered. In April 1896, Mrs. Wasson appointed Butte resident Jennie Stilwell Tallant (Mrs. Walter S.) to serve as organizing regent for a Butte DAR chapter. Among Montana Daughters, Tallant was fondly known as their "Grand Dame," for she hosted large teas and musicales, as well as state and chapter meetings in her spacious home. Butte was the logical city for the State Society DAR's first chapter because in the late 1800s (and beyond), the city was undisputedly the sole metropolis of Montana.

It was on a snowy Saturday, October 21, 2006, at 11:00 a.m. that DAR held a ceremony to dedicate a DAR insignia on the historic sign at 832 West Park Street to commemorate the home of their first chapter regent back in 1897. The ceremony was held in conjunction with the Silver Bow DAR chapter's replacement of the Pay Gold historic marker. *(See the "Pay Gold" chapter.)*

The wording on the historic sign installed by the U.S. Department of the Interior and Montana Historical Society is: "This property contributes to the Butte Historic District. Listed in the National Register of Historic Places by the United State Department of Interior in cooperation with the Montana Historical Society."

SOURCES
- Montana DAR website (www.montanadar.org/history-tidbits.html)
- *The Montana Standard* newspaper, Butte Montana, "A Place to Remember…," Oct. 20, 2006

*Another view of the Founder's House, 2018*

*Pay Gold DAR marker, 2017*

# 7. PAY GOLD

10 miles west of Butte
GPS coordinates: 46.00592| -112.649640

| | |
|---|---|
| **Commemorates** | Site of the first pay gold in Silver Bow County in the spring of 1864 |
| **Site Location** | Near the town of Nissler off the Butte-Anaconda highway near Silver Bow Creek |
| **Installed** | *Original*: August 24, 1931 |
| | *Refurbished and rededicated*: October 21, 2006 |
| **Wording** | "Pay gold was discovered in Silver Bow County near this site in July 1864 by Barker and party. To commemorate the event, this tablet was placed by Silver Bow Chapter Daughters of the American Revolution Butte, Montana. Original marker dedicated August 24, 1931. Restored and Rededicated 2006" |
| | At the foot of the monument, a separate plaque says, "Daughters of the American Revolution Silver Bow Chapter would like to acknowledge contributions from the following donors: Dennis R. Washington-Montana Resources, PPL Montana LLC, Dennis R. and Phyllis Washington, Northwestern Energy" |

# History

While Montana had earlier built a reputation as a site of significant gold deposits, the first discovery of "pay gold" (dirt containing enough gold ore to be worth extracting) in Silver Bow County was in 1864 by two prospectors (one named Butterworth Barker; the other's name is lost to history). The miners named the site the Missoula Lode. Other prospectors came, and by 1867 the population of the mining settlement reached 500 people. Water was scarce, however, and the town began to decline. By the 1870 census, only about 200 people remained. In that period, gold miners along Silver Bow Creek and its tributaries found an estimated $1.5 million of gold by 1867.

To commemorate the first discovery of gold in the county, the Silver Bow Chapter, NSDAR decided to install a marker near the discovery site. They received a bronze tablet donated by the Anaconda Copper Mining Company, and had it inset into a six-ton boulder donated by the Wendell Cannon Monument Works and placed close to the old town of Nissler. The marker was set 900 feet northeast of where the prospectors found the original gold at the site.

At 7:30 a.m. on August 24, 1931, the chapter conducted its dedication ceremonies "while the early sun's slanting rays played on the silvery arc of (Silver Bow) creek below." (Some sources say the ceremony was at 6:30 a.m.!) The early hour "was set on account of the heat." More than 150 people attended, including the President General of the National Society Daughters of the American Revolution, Mrs. Lowell Fletcher Hobart, who participated in the dedication ceremonies with Junior Honorary President General, Mrs. Grace L. Hall Brosseau.

According to newspaper accounts of the event, the original marker's wording was:

> *"Pay gold was discovered in Silver Bow County 900 feet southwest of here, July, 1804, by Butterworth Barker and party. To commemorate this event, this tablet was placed by Silver Bow Chapter, Daughters of the American Revolution, August 24, 1831."*

In addition to the many DAR officials and members attending, the local newspaper reported that Mrs. Laura Tolman Scott flew into town from nearby Dillon to attend the dedication via an airplane owned by Mr. and Mrs. Fred Woodside of Dillon. According to the paper:

> *Probably more enthusiastic than anyone present, Mrs. Scott, who has taken a prominent part in the marking of historical spots in Montana for many years, said that yesterday's memorial dedication was more interesting than any other sponsored by the D.A.R.*

In subsequent years, the bronze tablet was stolen and the boulder damaged.

Then, in 2006, the Silver Bow Chapter and State Highway Department placed a new marker affixed to the same granite boulder at the original spot on the south side of the old highway. The dedication of the replacement marker was on Saturday, October 21, 2006, at 11:00 a.m. Mrs. Iverna Lincoln Huntsman, State Regent of the Montana State Society DAR, was the featured speaker at the event. Other dignitaries were Past State Regent Shirley Groff, State Registrar and Silver Bow Regent JoAnn Piazzola, Constitution Week State Chair and past Silver Bow Regent Helen Brown, and past Silver Bow Regents Diane Sholey, Vicki Miller, Olive Boll, Jane Farrington and Wilda Bell.

SOURCES

- Historic monument records, Office of the Historian General, Washington D.C.
- *Record of Tablets and Markers Placed by Montana DAR 1908-1947*, by Mrs. Fred E. May
- *State Centennial History, MSSDAR*, by Iris McKinney Gray, Vol. V 1894-1994, pg. 39
- *Historical Sites Preserved and Markers Erected by MSSDAR and Its Chapters, 1899-1977*, by Mrs. R.V. Love and Mrs. E.E. Bruno
- *MSSDAR 1982-1984 Pictorial Supplement to Historic Events of 1894-1977*, by Mrs. R.V. Love, Mrs. Sidney Groff and Miss Lorene Burks
- *Daughters of the American Revolution Magazine*, November 1931, pg. 676
- *Daughters of the American Revolution Magazine*, January 1936, pg. 39
- US Dept. of the Interior, U.S. Geological Survey, "Maps Showing Locations of Mines and Prospects in the Butte 1x2 Quadrangle, Western Montana," by James E. Elliott, Jeffrey S. Loen, Kristine K. Wise, and Michael J. Blaskowski. Specific cite was Miller, R.N., 1973, Production History of the Butte District and Geological Function, Past and Present," in Miller, R.N., ed., Guidebook for the Butte Field Meeting of the Society of Economic Geologists: Society of Economic Geologists, U.S. Geological Survey, and the Anaconda Company, p. F-1 to F-10.
- *The Montana Standard* newspaper, Butte Montana, "Gold Discovery Commemorated: D.A.R. Head Presides at Dedication of Silver Bow Marker," Aug. 25, 1931, pg. 2
- *The Montana Standard* newspaper, Butte Montana, "Gold Discovery Will Be Marked: D.A.R. to Hold Program at Site in Silver Bow County Today," Aug. 24, 193, pg. 2
- *The Montana Standard* newspaper, Butte Montana, "Gold Discovery in Silver Bow Commemorated: D.A.R. President Presides at Dedication of Tablet Marking Historic Site," Aug. 25, 1931, pg. 1
- *The Montana Standard* newspaper, Butte Montana, "75-year-old D.A.R. Lady Flies From Dillon to Be Present at Dedication Here," Aug. 25, 1931, pg. 1
- *The Montana Standard* newspaper, Butte Montana, "Aged D.A.R. Member Flies to Dedication: Takes Trip Down Mine," Aug. 25, 1931, pg. 2
- *The Montana Standard* newspaper, Butte Montana, "A Place to Remember: 'Pay Gold' Monument Dedication Saturday", Oct. 20, 2006, pg. 1

*August 25, 1931, Montana Standard newspaper*

*1999 and 1908 Spanish-American War Veterans Memorial markers (above), 2017 Photo in 1909 DAR American Monthly Magazine (below)*

WORK OF THE CHAPTERS.  1207

marker which is a native boulder, only the face is polished and these surmounted by the insignia and the date 1908, the following inscription is placed:

Stone Coping Erected by Silver Bow Chapter, Butte, Montana.

"This plot is enclosed by Silver Bow Chapter, Daughters of the American Revolution, as a memorial to the Montana soldiers who lost their lives in the Spanish-American War."

# 8. Spanish-American War Veterans Memorial

Butte
GPS coordinates: 45.98580899 | -112.54260152

| | |
|---|---|
| **Commemorates** | Soldiers who served in the Spanish-American War |
| **Site Location** | In an overlapping plot spanning both Mount Moriah Cemetery and Catholic Cemetery, off South Montana Street, Butte |
| **Installed** | *Original*: May 29, 1908 |
| | *Second marker and rededicated*: May 8, 1999 |
| **Wording** | *Original:* "1908 This plot is enclosed by Silver Bow Chapter Daughters of the American Revolution as a memorial to the Montana soldiers who lost their lives in the Spanish American War" |
| | *Second marker*: "This plot is enclosed by Silver Bow Chapter, Daughters of the American Revolution, as a memorial to the men and women who served in the Spanish-American War. Dedicated 8 May 1999" |

# History

This was the first historical marker to be placed by Montana DAR chapters. It honored Montana Spanish-American War soldiers who sacrificed their lives in that war. As originally installed, the memorial was surrounded by granite curbing, with granite posts at intervals supporting iron chains, and a tall flag pole. At the base of the flag pole, DAR installed a large granite boulder with a carved inscription.

While the memorial was finally installed at sundown on the evening of May 29, 1908, Silver Bow Chapter, NSDAR had begun raising funds back in about 1901. In that year, the chapter decided to honor Montana volunteers who died in the Spanish-American War by erecting a bronze drinking fountain near the new post office building planned for Butte. State Regent Antoinette Van Hook Browne reported to the 1901 DAR Continental Congress that:

> *...over $300 has been raised by the untiring efforts of the Chapter members for the purpose of erecting to the memory of their countrymen a drinking fountain in the city of Butte, which shall be both useful and ornamental, and which shall be an everlasting memorial*

By 1904, the chapter added another $265 to the fund by hosting a Revolutionary Ball and the "Committee on Fountain" persuaded the city council to donate $1,000. Then, trouble. When Butte's city council was enjoined from paying the monies promised, the chapter hired Mrs. Henri J. (Ella Knowles) Haskell, Montana's first woman lawyer and female attorney general (also the chapter regent) to sue for the promised payment. Embarrassingly, the fountain's sculptor was ready to proceed with the project. But in September 1905, the chapter learned that the District Court had made an adverse decision.

The chapter abandoned the fountain in favor of another way to honor the war dead with the fund, now grown to $700. They learned that a 72-foot by 56-foot plot, lying partly in the Mount Moriah Cemetery and the Catholic Cemetery adjacent to Butte, had been reserved for Spanish-American War veterans. The memorial committee decided to install their memorial there, after eight years of struggle.

The May 29, 1908, dedication ceremonies included marching war veterans and an address by the mayor.

Ninety-one years later, the original incised stone marker had become almost illegible, but as it had been declared a national historic site by DAR, a new monument with revised wording was installed at a cost of $800 raised by the local Silver Bow Chapter.

The chapter reports that members are now working on repairing the deteriorated granite enclosure around the plot and the plot itself. This effort is expected to be completed in 2020.

### SOURCES

- Historic monument records, Office of the Historian General, Wash. D.C.
- *Record of Tablets and Markers Placed by Montana DAR 1908-1947*, by Mrs. Fred E. May
- *State Centennial History, MSSDAR*, by Iris McKinney Gray, Vol. V 1894-1994
- *Historical Sites Preserved and Markers Erected by MSSDAR and Its Chapters 1899-1977*, by Mrs. R.V. Love and Mrs. E.E. Bruno
- *MSSDAR 1982-1984 Pictorial Supplement to Historic Events of 1894-1977*, by Mrs. R.V. Love, Mrs. Sidney Groff and Miss Lorene Burks
- *DAR American Monthly Magazine*, Sept. 1909, pps. 798-801
- *DAR American Monthly Magazine*, Dec. 1909, pps. 1206-1207
- *The Montana Standard* newspaper, Butte Montana, "DAR Will Dedicate Veterans' Monument," May 1, 1999, pg. 5
- *The Butte Weekly* newspaper, Butte Montana, "War Monument Dedicated in May 9 DAR Ceremony," May 12, 1999
- *The Anaconda Standard* newspaper, Anaconda Montana, "God's Acre Dedicated to Boys of Last War," May 30, 1908, pg. 5

*Dillon's Founding DAR marker (above) and site (below), 2017*

# 9. Dillon's Founding

Dillon
GPS coordinates: 45.215775 | -112.635778

| | |
|---|---|
| **Commemorates** | Dillon's founding |
| **Site Location** | St. James Episcopal Church, 203 E. Glendale St., (Washington Street side), by door to the church's guild hall |
| **Installed** | September 25, 1930 |
| **Wording** | "1880-1930 This tablet marks the site of the first public school building which was also used for the first court house-theatre and library in Dillon. Dedicated to the pioneers of the valley on the fiftieth anniversary of the founding of Dillon. Placed by Beaverhead Chapter Daughters of the American Revolution" |

## History

The DAR-installed marker on St. James Episcopal Church marks the remnant building that was the city of Dillon's first courthouse and one of Dillon's first public school buildings, its first theater, and first library. The bronze marker was presented by Beaverhead Chapter,

NSDAR and installed at 10:45 a.m. on September 25, 1930, as part of Dillon's 50th anniversary celebration. *(Note: some historic sources say September 30.)*

In typical DAR fashion, the ceremony began with a bugle call, followed by the assembled crowd singing "America," and then speeches. Mrs. John F. Bishop, a Montana pioneer, unveiled the plaque and history professor R.E. Albright from Montana State Normal College (now University of Montana Western), a descendant of a Revolutionary War soldier, gave the address.

Dillon was founded by Union Pacific Railroad president Sidney Dillon, who liked the location because of its proximity to gold mines in the area. Silver was the first ore discovered in the Dillon area, followed by gold (discovered at Grasshopper Creek in 1862), both of which saw a flood of immigrants to the Beaverhead Valley. Dillon was a central location for transporting goods to nearby mining boomtowns like Bannack, Argenta, Glen, and Virginia City. The last real gold rush in the area, near Argenta in 1920, lasted for 30 years.

Because of its location near a lesser-used church entrance, even many Dillon natives do not know the DAR plaque exists.

SOURCES

- Historic monument records, Office of the Historian General, Washington D.C.
- *State Centennial History, MSSDAR*, by Iris McKinney Gray, Vol. V 1894-1994
- *Historical Sites Preserved and Markers Erected by MSSDAR and Its Chapters 1899-1977*, by Mrs. R.V. Love and Mrs. E.E. Bruno
- *MSSDAR 1982-1984 Pictorial Supplement to Historic Events of 1894-1977*, by Mrs. R.V. Love, Mrs. Sidney Groff and Miss Lorene Burks
- *Dillon Examiner* newspaper, Dillon Montana, "Courthouse Marker Will be Unveiled," Sept. 24, 1930

*Historic photo of the two-story wood frame structure hastily constructed during spring 1881 for Beaverhead Cunty offices. The second floor housed Dillon's school, used until 1883 when a new brick school building was constructed. (Beaverhead County Museum photo)*

*Pathfinder Tribute DAR marker (above) and site (below), 2017*

# 10. Pathfinder Tribute

Dillon
GPS coordinates: 45.217124 | -112.638244

| | |
|---|---|
| **Commemorates** | Passage of the Lewis and Clark Expedition through Beaverhead County |
| **Site Location** | Railway depot lawn, facing the tracks of the Oregon Short Line Railroad (later Union Pacific Railroad) |
| **Installed** | June 14, 1928 |
| **Wording** | "The Lewis and Clark Expedition passed this way going west August, 1805 and returning July, 1806. 'Though the Pathfinder may die; the paths remain open.' Beaverhead Chapter Daughters of the American Revolution. June 14, 1928" |

## History

At 7:00 p.m. on Flag Day, June 14, 1928, the Beaverhead Chapter, NSDAR held a ceremony that unveiled a "handsome Lewis & Clark marker jointly donated by the Anaconda Copper Mining Company and the Oregon Short Line Railroad." The bronze marker was inset into a large granite boulder donated by the Oregon Short Line Railroad and brought to Dillon from the mountains by Birch Creek. The local newspaper proudly noted that the bronze marker was "constructed by Montana workmen from Montana-mined metals…"

The ceremony, watched by hundreds, began with a bugle call, followed by all of the audience singing "America" and "The Star Spangled Banner." History professor R.E. Albright of Montana State Normal College (now University of Montana Western) "gave an interesting and detailed outline of the passage of the Lewis & Clark Expedition through Beaverhead County, particularly the Beaverhead Valley." The professor:

> …*called attention to the fact that the description of the valley as given in the journals of the expedition still holds good in many respects. Bearings taken by Clark from Lover's Leap (a bluff just north of Dillon) were remarkably exact.*

Mrs. Laura Tolman Scott, state chair of the Historic Spots Committee of Montana DAR, dedicated the monument and presented it to the city and its schools. The pathfinder quote on the marker is hers.

While passenger trains ran through Dillon, the memorial was visible to passengers from its spot on the rail depot lawn. Although passenger trains no longer run through Dillon, the marker remains in its original spot, which is now in front of the Beaverhead County Museum where it continues to be seen by passersby yet today.

The marker was rededicated on August 9, 1945, in a 7:30 p.m. celebration of the 140th anniversary of the Lewis and Clark Expedition. The ceremony, led by the Dillon chapter of the American Pioneer Trails Association, included principal speaker Professor Rush Jordan of the Montana State Normal College, also chair of the Beaverhead Chapter of the Pioneer Trails Association. Other speakers were Dr. Sheldon E. Davis ("A Fitting Memorial at Beaverhead Rock"), John Collins ("The Beaverhead County Museum"), W.R. Allen for the Beaverhead Mining Association ("Historical Markers in Beaverhead County"), Mayor O.T. Vandegrift ("Local Park Areas"), and County Commissioner Archie Henneberry ("Preservation of Bannack Historical Site").

The Beaverhead DAR chapter of Dillon, founded on March 10, 1917, merged with Butte's Silver Bow Chapter on April 18, 1998.

SOURCES

- Historic monument records, Office of the Historian General, Washington D.C.
- *Record of Tablets and Markers Placed by Montana DAR 1908-1947*, by Mrs. Fred E. May
- *State Centennial History, MSSDAR*, by Iris McKinney Gray, Vol. V 1894-1994
- *Historical Sites Preserved and Markers Erected by MSSDAR and Its Chapters, 1899-1977*, by Mrs. R.V. Love and Mrs. E.E. Bruno
- *MSSDAR 1982-1984 Pictorial Supplement to Historic Events of 1894-1977*, by Mrs. R.V. Love, Mrs. Sidney Groff and Miss Lorene Burks
- *The Dillon Examiner* newspaper, Dillon Montana, "Ceremonies to be Held on O.S.L. Depot Lawn," June 13, 1928, pg. 1
- *The Dillon Examiner* newspaper, Dillon Montana, "Lewis and Clark Marker Was Unveiled Thursday," June 20, 1928
- *The Montana Standard* newspaper, Butte Montana, "Beaverhead County Residents to Commemorate the Passage of Lewis and Clark Party in Region," Aug. 5, 1945, pg. 11

*Historic Bannack DAR marker (above) and site (below), 2017*

# 11. Historic Bannack

25 miles southwest of Dillon, off MT-278 West
GPS coordinates: 45.162393 | -112.998877

| | |
|---|---|
| **Commemorates** | Montana's oldest capital and the site near where Captain Clark passed in July 1806 on the return trip from the Pacific Northwest |
| **Site Location** | *Original*: in front of the Meade Hotel |
| | *Current*: off the parking lot just west of the Visitor Center, a National Historic Landmark and Montana State Park |
| **Installed** | September 7, 1925 |
| **Wording** | "Bannack. Lewis and Clark Trail 1806. First Important Gold Camp 1862. Scene of Vigilante Activities 1863. First Capital Territory of Montana 1864-1865. First County Seat of Beaverhead County 1864-1881. In grateful memory of the early pioneers who founded our commonwealth. Erected by Montana State Society Daughters of the American Revolution 1925" |

# History

On September 7, 1925, 150 people braved muddy roads and threatening grey clouds to attend the annual DAR Labor Day picnic at which a bronze marker was placed in front of Bannack's Meade Hotel. The original marker was made of "native Montana copper and related ores" donated to the Montana Society DAR (Beaverhead Chapter, NSDAR) by the Anaconda Copper Mining Company. At 1:30 p.m., the sun came out and after a picnic lunch, a bugle call sounded, followed by an invocation and singing of "The Star Spangled Banner."

In accepting the marker for the state on behalf of Governor John E. Erickson, David Hilger, State Librarian of the Historical Society, commended DAR for "splendid services in placing markers at historical spots in Montana and for assisting in collecting and preserving a truthful history of the state." Congressman Scott Leavitt told of the "characters who devoted their fortunes, their efforts and their lives to instill obedience to law and order," while former Congressman Washington J. McCormick "recited interesting anecdotes which he learned from his father, a member of the first territorial legislature, which was held on the spot marked by the tablet."

The territory in and around Bannack is deeply historic. It has been under the sovereignty of three flags–Spain, France, and the American Stars and Stripes. It has also been under separate territories and a state government. Captain William Clark passed through or near Bannack July 1806 on the Expedition's return trip from the Pacific Northwest.

Bannack, which took its name from the Bannock Indians, came into existence in 1862 and quickly became known as one of the wildest mining camps in the Northwest. John White and other Colorado prospectors discovered gold there in what came to be known as

"Grasshopper Diggins." Many followed and by January 1862, Bannack's population was 500. Many of these men were wild and ruthless. Henry Plummer, who was elected sheriff, was later hanged by the Vigilantes who accused him of being the ringleader of a gang of violent bandits.

When the Montana Territory was established in 1864, Bannack was its first territorial capital. Sidney Edgerton, named governor by President Abraham Lincoln, assumed office in Bannack as the First Territorial Governor and resided in Bannack during his term of office. The first legislative session ever held in the territory convened at Bannack during the winter of 1864, meeting in the governor's cabin. In 1866, however, the territorial capital was moved to Virginia City until being permanently moved to Helena in 1877.

It was DAR that saved Bannack. In 1953, DAR member Mrs. Elfreda Woodside decided to purchase the rapidly-deteriorating mining camp of Bannack. With the aid of a sizeable loan from a banking friend, she secured the famed Gold Gulch from a defunct mining company, and the following year donated it to the state of Montana. She subsequently sparked campaigns that resulted in Bannack being designated a National Historic Landmark and later a State Park. In 1962, she chaired the 100th Anniversary of Bannack's Centennial Celebration of the discovery of gold in the Montana Territory.

DAR's marker was moved to the parking lot at the entry of Bannack State Park in 1989 or 1990 when the county abandoned the old road. This is a National Historic Landmark and a Register of Historic Places site.

**SOURCES**

- Historic monument records, Office of the Historian General, Washington D.C.
- *Record of Tablets and Markers Placed by Montana DAR 1908-1947*, by Mrs. Fred E. May
- *State Centennial History, MSSDAR*, by Iris McKinney Gray, Vol. V 1894-1994
- *Historical Sites Preserved and Markers Erected by MSSDAR and Its Chapters 1899-1977*, by Mrs. R.V. Love and Mrs. E.E. Bruno
- *MSSDAR 1982-1984 Pictorial Supplement to Historic Events of 1894-1977*, by Mrs. R.V. Love, Mrs. Sidney Groff and Miss Lorene Burks
- *Dillon Examiner* newspaper, Dillon Montana, "DAR to Erect Bronze Tablet at Bannack," Aug. 28, 1925
- *Dillon Examiner* newspaper, Dillon Montana, "Historical Old Bannack is Marked," Sept. 2, 1925

*Dedication of DAR historical marker at Bannack, 1925*
*With permission, Montana Historical Society Research Center Photography Archives 957-637*

*DAR monument Sacajawea Memorial–Armstead, 2017*

# 12. Sacajawea Memorial- Armstead

20 miles south of Dillon, off I-15
GPS coordinates: 44.99788755 | -112.85596982

| | |
|---|---|
| **Commemorates** | Indian guide Sacajawea |
| **Site Location** | *Original*: one-half mile north of Armstead |
| | *Current:* east side Clark Canyon Dam campground |
| **Installed** | November 15, 1915 |
| **Wording** | "In commemoration of Sacajawea who guided Lewis and Clark through this, the land of her childhood and capture. On August 17th 1805 she rejoined her tribe near this site. The services she rendered the expedition were invaluable. This tablet was erected by the Montana Daughters of the American Revolution, 1915" |

# History

Montana State Society DAR arranged for a pageant and dedication ceremony to present the Sacajawea Memorial marker at Armstead for Monday, August 30, 1915. But since the bronze marker did not arrive in time from New York, DAR decided to hold the pageant with the marker boulder in place, but without the bronze plaque. A special train carried a group of 300 from Dillon to Armstead for the event, which started with a picnic. Attendees were advised to wear "a costume that will be comfortable for a short hike to the top of the hill."

Newspapers of the day reported a "Celebration at Armstead," starting at 1:15 p.m., complete with picnics, pageantry, and music by the Dillon Military Band. The DAR pageant depicted historic scenes and included Shoshone Indians from the Lemhi reservation, descendants of those whom Lewis and Clark had met. The program included several dances: "Spirit of Adventure," by a group of Dillon girls and "Owl Dance," by Campfire Girls of Sacajawea Camp of Dillon. That evening, attendees were invited to a dance in Armstead.

Later that fall, on Monday, November 15, 1915, Montana DAR held the delayed ceremony to place the bronze DAR marker at the Two Forks of the Missouri River, at the Oregon Short Line railway depot at Armstead. The marker, donated by the Anaconda Copper Mining Company, was installed in a large granite boulder and placed on "a specially prepared lawn just south of the Oregon Short Line station at Armstead, a thriving community south of Dillon…"

Former Senator W.A. Clark presented the tablet to DAR and was the principal speaker at the unveiling ceremonies. His address was reported to have been greatly enjoyed by all, and his personal reminiscences of early days in Montana "delighted the many old timers present." The senator arrived via the morning Oregon Short Line train to which the senator's private rail car was attached.

C.A. Brigham called the gathering to order and drew the speakers to the platform in the specially-decorated hall: DAR State Regent Mrs. E.A. Morley, Mrs. Clinton H. Moore, Senator Clark, Olin D. Wheeler of St. Paul, a Lewis and Clark Expedition author, and Rev. Edward Smith (Armstead). "One of the most charming numbers on the program, the singing of the Sacajawea lullaby by Mrs. Clarence Holt, attired as Sacajawea, and singing to what represented a little Indian papoose asleep."

DAR member Mrs. Clinton H. Moore, a Montana historian, presented the memorial to Armstead which was accepted by Mrs. J.W. (Laura Tolman) Scott.

Historians say this site was the pivotal point of the Expedition's journey because without their loyal Indian guide, Sacajawea, the Expedition might have ended there. Lewis and Clark had for months toiled up the Missouri River, portaged around the Great Falls, through the Gates of the Mountains, and the Three Forks of the Missouri. They then chose the Jefferson River to continue their journey. But they found their heavily laden canoes increasingly difficult to navigate. On August 17, 1805, they reached the Two Forks of the Missouri (now the Red Rock River and Horse Prairie Creek). The river they had been following divided itself into two.

This was journey's end as far as they could go with canoes and the most serious obstacle of the entire journey. Fortunately, a band of Shoshone Indians rode up and Sacajawea recognized her brother among them. The Indians furnished the Expedition with horses and guides for the difficult trek over the Continental Divide and the mountains on the other side. The Lewis and Clark Expedition camped at the original site on August 17-24, 1805, and Captain Clark also camped here on his return from the Pacific Northwest in 1806.

The original DAR marker site, one-half mile north of Armstead, is now submerged under Clark Canyon Dam waters. The marker and its boulder were moved to the east side campground of Clark Canyon Dam in the early 1960s.

This bronze DAR tablet is similar in design to the one erected by DAR at Three Forks. *(See Sacajawea Memorial-Three Forks chapter.)*

**SOURCES**
- Historic monument records, Office of the Historian General, Washington D.C.
- *Records of Tablets and Markers Placed by Montana DAR 1908-1947*, by Mrs. Fred E. May
- *State Centennial History, MSSDAR*, by Iris McKinney Gray, Vol. V 1894-1994
- *Historical Sites Preserved and Markers Erected by MSSDAR and Its Chapters, 1899-1977*, by Mrs. R.V. Love and Mrs. E.E. Bruno
- *MSSDAR 1982-1984 Pictorial Supplement to Historic Events of 1894-1977*, by Mrs. R.V. Love, Mrs. Sidney Groff and Miss Lorene Burks
- *The Dillon Examiner* newspaper, Dillon Montana, "Celebration at Armstead," August 25, 1915
- *The Dillon Examiner* newspaper, Dillon Montana, "Sacajawea Pageant is Glowing Tribute by People of Armstead," Sept. 3, 1915, pps. 1, 9, 10
- *The Butte Miner* newspaper, Butte Montana, photo: "Senator W.A. Clark Shown Standing Beside the Sacajawea Tablet," Nov. 16, 1915, pps. 1, 3, 7
- *DAR American Spirit Magazine*, May 1916, pps. 351-352

*The Butte Miner newspaper, November 16, 1915*

*Southern Gateway marker site, 2017*

# 13. SOUTHERN GATEWAY

8 miles south of Dillon

GPS coordinates: 45.12961776 | -112.74087252

| | |
|---|---|
| **Commemorates** | Historic route |
| **Site Location** | Barretts Station off I-15 |
| **Installed** | *Original*: September 23, 1935 |
| | *Moved and rededicated*: September 7, 1991 |
| **Wording** | "Beaverhead Canyon Gateway (Ryan's Canyon). The waters of the Beaverhead River opened this southern gateway to Montana through which have passed: Ancient Indian Trail<br>Lewis and Clark Expedition 1805-1806<br>First Missionary, Father DeSmet 1840<br>Great Beaverhead Wagon Toll Road 1866-1880 (chartered by James Ryan and William Sturgis)<br>First Railroad into Montana, the Utah and Northern 1880<br>On this site stood the old toll house, toll gate and bridge nearby, Sturgis Post Office and Junction 1868, Ryan Post Office 1869 and T.M. Barrett Store 1874.<br>Erected by Beaverhead Chapter Daughters of the American Revolution A.D. 1935" |

# History

Originally located across the Beaverhead River from Rattlesnake Cliffs, this tablet commemorates the exceptional history of the site–Beaverhead Canyon Gateway's ancient Indian trails, the Lewis and Clark Expedition to the Pacific Coast, the path of Father DeSmet in 1840, the first railroad into Montana, and the Great Beaverhead Wagon Toll Road (1868-1880) which opened traffic to Virginia City. The area, called "the Southern Gateway into Montana," is said to be exceeded in history only by Fort Benton.

In 1805, the Lewis and Clark Expedition passed through this route going west. The Expedition also returned by this route in 1806, when Captain Clark and his party came back to recover a cache of guns and ammunition left at Camp Fortunate when they journeyed west. Clark and his men continued homeward through the Big Hole over the Bozeman Pass and down the Yellowstone River to its mouth where the entire command of Lewis and Clark was reunited.

When the DAR marker was originally dedicated at 10:30 a.m. on September 23, 1935, DAR President General Mrs. William A. (Florence) Becker, DAR Organizing Secretary General Mrs. William H. (Helena) Pouch, DAR National Vice Chair of Historical Research Mrs. Laura Tolman Scott, and Montana Governor Frank H. Cooney and his wife (a "native daughter of Beaverhead County") attended the ceremony, "witnessed by scores of Montana and Idaho people." Mrs. Kate Sturgis Poindexter Linn, daughter of William Sturgis who is mentioned on the marker, also attended. Historian Dr. R.E. Albright delivered the historical address. DAR State Regent Mrs. Elfreda (J. Fred) Woodside formally presented the marker to the State of Montana. It consisted of a bronze tablet donated by the Anaconda

Copper Mining Company, installed in an eight-foot monument of native rock masonry by Hugh Gray of Dillon.

Governor Cooney's remarks that day included the following:

*The trips that once took weeks and months are now made in hours. The toll road of the olden days has vanished with the oxcart and the covered wagon, the stage coach and the mule teams. Cities and towns and villages have sprung up and the points once separated by impassable barriers are brought into neighborly close connection with each other with the bands of steel and the modern railroad trains, bus lines, automobile caravans and trucks. We can stand today on these hilltops where once our pioneer fathers and mothers crouched and gazed with fear and trepidation for dangers to be avoided ... Now we look calmly down on peaceful valleys and calmly scan the horizon as long trains pass ... the cars loaded with copper, lead, zinc, wheat, rye, apples, cherries, sheep, cattle, wool and the products of our dairies are whisked away to meet the needs of the East. This marker today stands as a mute evidence of the passing of the old and the welcoming of the new.*

Fifty-six years later, after a state highway route changed its placement at the foot of Rattlesnake Cliffs, local historic preservationist and DAR State Regent Mrs. Elfreda (J. Fred) Woodside ensured that the original DAR bronze tablet was refurbished and moved east to a beautifully-crafted rock wall built to protect it at its current state highway campground location.

The monument was rededicated on September 7, 1991. Honorary State Regent Woodside, four days from her 94th birthday, attended the ceremony.

SOURCES

- Historic monument records, Office of the Historian General, Washington D.C.
- *Record of Tablets and Markers Placed by Montana DAR 1908-1947*, by Mrs. Fred E. May
- *State Centennial History, MSSDAR*, by Iris McKinney Gray, Vol. V 1894-1994
- *Historical Sites Preserved and Markers Erected by MSSDAR and Its Chapters 1899-1977*, by Mrs. R.V. Love and Mrs. E.E. Bruno
- *MSSDAR 1982-1984 Pictorial Supplement to Historic Events of 1894-1977*, by Mrs. R.V. Love, Mrs. Sidney Groff and Miss Lorene Burks
- *The Dillon Examiner* newspaper, Dillon Montana, "National Leader Will be Here Next Monday," Sept. 18, 1935
- *The Dillon Examiner* newspaper, Dillon Montana, "D.A.R. Head is Dillon Visitor: Governor Cooney Also Guest at Dedication of Marker Monday," Sept. 25, 1935, pg. 1
- Unknown newspaper dated Sept. 23, 1935, "D.A.R. to Mark the Site of Famous Old Pioneer Road"

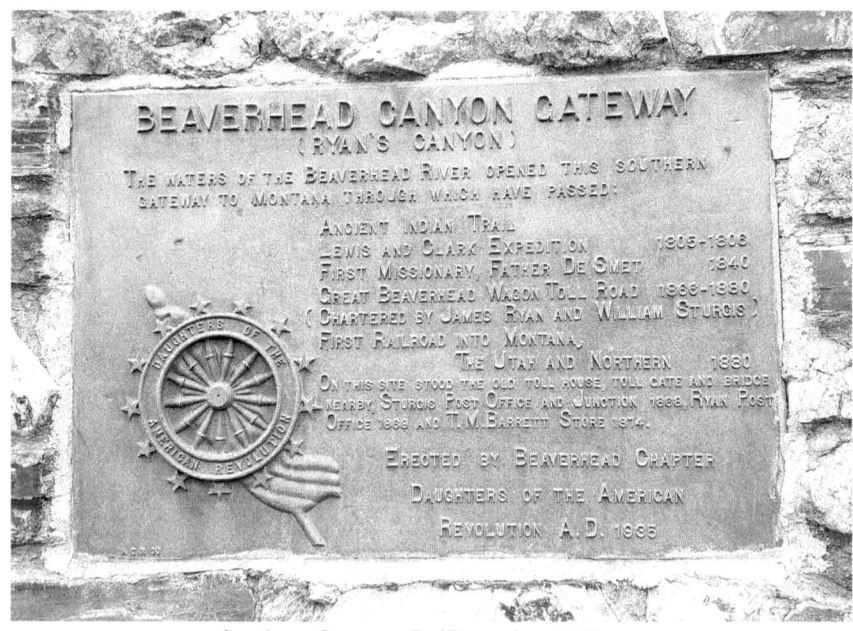

*Southern Gateway DAR marker, 2017*

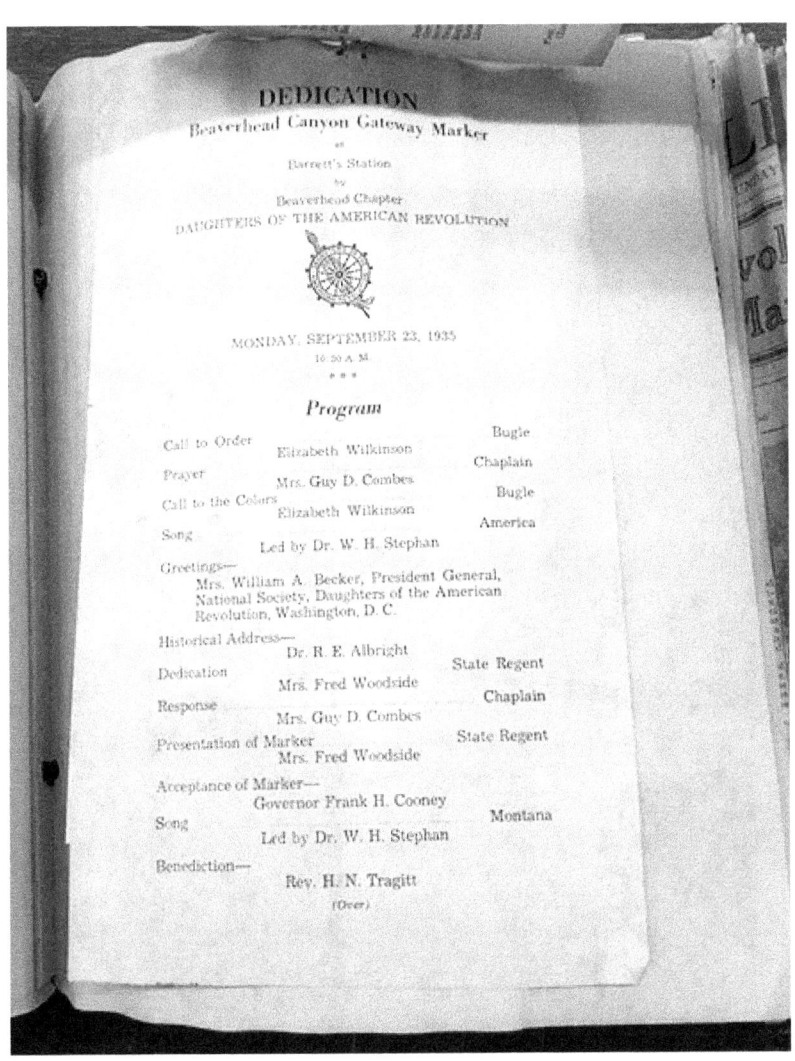

*1935 dedication program for Southern Gateway DAR marker, 2017*

*Old Fort Benton Blockhouse site, 2018*

# 14. Old Fort Benton Blockhouse

Fort Benton

GPS coordinates: 47.821388 | -110.663055

| | |
|---|---|
| **Commemorates** | Historic fur-trading post and blockhouse restoration |
| **Site Location** | Fort Benton, a National Historic Landmark |
| **Installed** | August 2019 (planned) |
| **Wording** | "Old Fort Benton. This block house stands as the only building at historic Fort Benton built during the North American fur trade. Originally named Fort Lewis, Pierre Chouteau, Jr. and Company established this site as a fur fort in 1846. The fort was renamed Fort Benton on Christmas Day of 1850 in honor of Missouri Senator Thomas Hart Benton. The blockhouse was originally constructed of logs, and during the 1850's was gradually reconstructed of adobe. The thick adobe walls replaced the exterior logs around the block house while the original interior log structure and roof remained in place. |

During the decline of the fur trade industry, the Northwest Fur Company purchased the fort in 1865 and was later occupied by the United States Army. After 1847, the military moved into quarters in town, and by 1877 the fort buildings were completely abandoned. By the early 1900's most of the fort's structures had disappeared and this historic block house stood in grave danger of collapsing.

In 1907 Representative T.A. Cummings persuaded the Montana Legislature to appropriate $800 to restore and preserve Old Fort Benton. National Society Daughters of the American Revolution members Antoinette Van Hook Browne, Ella Lydia Arnold Renisch, and Eliza A. Sturtevant Condon were appointed as Trustees to administer the funding. Thanks to the prompt action of the Montana Daughters, the walls and roof of the block house were stabilized and stucco was applied to the exterior in 1908.

Today, this Block House is recognized as one of the earliest examples of historic preservation in Montana and as the only original building in the oldest continuously occupied Anglo-American settlement in Montana.

Presented by Montana State Society Daughters of the American Revolution August 2019"

# History

This is the site of the Montana State Society DAR's first state-wide project as well as its most recent historical marker.

The fur trading post of Fort Benton was first established in 1846 by the American Fur Company. The Blackfeet Indians asked the

American Fur Company's agent at Fort Lewis, Alexander Culbertson, to relocate the fort to the north side of the Missouri River and a broad grassy river bottom on the north side a few miles downriver was selected as the site of Fort Benton. It was to be the last fur trading fort on the Upper Missouri. Fort Lewis' log buildings, walls, and bastions were dismantled and floated to their new site. By the spring of 1847, the last structures were rafted down the Missouri to form the new trading post. But Alexander Culbertson was not satisfied with his fort. While at Fort Laramie he had seen the adobe buildings of the Southwest, and felt adobe would offer more protection against the Upper Missouri's extreme weather than could logs. Reconstruction of the fort using adobe bricks made of Missouri River clay began in the fall of 1848. A two-story dwelling for Major Culbertson was the first building completed. Reconstruction was completed in 1860 when the trade store was rebuilt. The American Fur Company sold the fort in 1865 to the Northwest Fur Company.

According to the Fort Benton *River Press* newspaper on June 9, 1976, "The Block House, built in 1850 of sun dried adobe bricks, is one of the oldest in Montana, exceptions being, possibly one of two of the missions in western Montana."

Since 1864, the settlement around the old fort had been the hub of the territory's supplies coming in for mining camps and raw gold going out. Later it was the center for shipping wool to eastern mills. From 1869 to its abandonment in 1882, the U.S. Army maintained a garrison at the fort to protect shipments. After the army left, Fort Assinniboine near Havre was left to protect the region. *(See Fort Assinniboine chapter.)* Soon, railroads ended navigation on the Missouri River to Fort Benton.

Old Fort Benton's story is linked to Montana's second DAR State Regent, Mrs. David G. (Antoinette Van Hook) Browne. In February 1899, the DAR National Board of Management appointed Mrs. Browne as State Regent. The new State Regent had personal history with the old fort–the Brownes for many years lived directly opposite the buildings of the abandoned military garrison which had given the town of Fort Benton its name.

While efforts to restore the old fort covered quite a few years, they had their beginning during Mrs. Browne's State Regent term (1899-1901). In 1907, she was instrumental in getting the 10th Montana Legislative Assembly to appropriate $800 for the fort's restoration. Governor Joseph H. Toole appointed Mrs. Browne Chair of the Trustees for both property and funds, along with Ella Lydia Arnold (Mrs. E.H.) Renisch (Butte) and Eliza A. Sturtevant Condon (Helena) as the other two trustees.

The board quickly started active work on the project and in October 1907, Jere Sullivan, chair of the Chouteau County Board of Commissioners, issued to the Trustees of the Old Fort a quitclaim deed for the former interests of W.S. Wetzel and Sarah E. Eastman for the consideration of one dollar. In only a few days, this was followed by a similar deed to the trustees given by Mr. and Mrs. Charles E. Duer.

Mrs. Browne and the Montana Daughters found active support from local Fort Benton women. A Ladies' Improvement Society of 73 ladies organized itself on November 7, 1907, at the Grand Union Hotel and formed four committees–Committee on Fencing, Committee on Hall, Committee on Lawn, and Committee on Entertainment.

In May 1908, as part of its efforts to fund the project, the Oro Fino Chapter, NSDAR sponsored a concert "for the purpose of raising money for a gateway to the park surrounding the old fort."

The debris was cleared, the old northeast blockhouse restored by the use of adobe bricks and a cement covering, and the buildings were strengthened for safety. A driveway with walks and a gateway were built to mark the site, which was landscaped with grass and trees. Thus Old Fort Park came into existence. On April 4, 1918, the property was turned over to the town of Fort Benton to be kept and preserved as a park.

In 1929, the Montana Legislature designated Old Fort Benton as a site for a State Memorial to Lewis and Clark. In 1931, "the Memorial Park was well under way and in it a tree was planted for each Chouteau County man who gave his life in World War I."

Sun-dried adobe bricks are unable to withstand Montana's weather and by the 1940s only the preserved northeast bastion and a partial wall from the Engages' Quarters remained. Then, in 1946, a high wind blew over one of the remaining walls of the old fort, partially rebuilt of the original bricks with concrete added for strength. The wind damaged that section and a fragment of another wall, which were protected by wire enclosures by the Fort Benton Community Improvement Association around 1931.

Joining the 1800s-era northeast blockhouse, the local River and Plains Society (Upper Missouri River Museum) rebuilt the southwest blockhouse at Fort Benton that had been missing since the 1890s. Adding a new blockhouse was to help protect the historic northeast blockhouse, which was generally kept closed because visitors broke off and took pieces of its adobe. The "new" blockhouse, a fortified corner tower, would have held gunpowder and weapons, with slits for firing from and thick walls for protection, although the traders had good relations with the tribes and weren't attacked. Before rebuilding the blockhouse, a 2016 archeological study was done to determine where exactly it had stood. Besides finding the blockhouse layout, volunteers also unearthed a glass bead from Venice (Italy), nails, glass, clay pipe stems, seed beads, and bones.

DAR's most recent involvement with the site traces to Montana State Regent Catherine T. Lane, who in 2014, along with Honorary State Regents Shirley Groff and JoAnn Piazzola, began looking into the possibility of working with Fort Benton to place a DAR marker at the fort. The team of three realized that after all the years of DAR involvement with Old Fort Benton, there was no DAR marker recognizing the restoration and preservation efforts of past Montana Daughters.

To help finance a DAR marker, most Montana chapters and members contributed to this project, to culminate in an August 2019 statewide marker ceremony. The DAR marker will be placed close to the entrance of the blockhouse inside the Fort Benton stockade and visible to all as they enter the historic block house.

Currently, Fort Benton is a National Historic Landmark and part of the Old Forts Trail, an international heritage tourism trail connecting seven historic forts in Montana, Alberta, and Saskatchewan.

SOURCES
- *Record of Tablets and Markers Placed by Montana DAR 1908-1947*, by Mrs. Fred E. May
- *State Centennial History*, MSSDAR, by Iris McKinney Gray, Vol. V 1894-1994
- *Restoration of Old Fort Benton, in DAR Markers in Montana*, compiled by Mrs. E.E. Bruno, State Co-Chair DAR Markers Committee, 1976-1978

- *American Monthly Magazine* (DAR), July-Dec. 1907, pps. 244-245
- *American Monthly Magazine* (DAR), Sept. 1909, pps. 798-801
- *Butte Miner* newspaper, Butte Montana, "For Citizens of the Future: Daughters of Revolution Want Historic Sites Preserved, Unanimously Sanction Restoring Ft. Benton," Nov. 3, 1907, pg. 5
- *Great Falls Tribune* newspaper, Great Falls Montana, "For the Restoration of Old Fort Benton," Nov. 3, 1907, pg. 4
- *The River Press* newspaper, Fort Benton Montana, "To Preserve Old Fort – Ladies Form Organization That Will Assist in the Work," November 13, 1907
- *Great Falls Daily Tribune* newspaper, Great Falls Montana, "Preservation of Old Fort," May 10, 1908, pg. 2
- *The River Press* newspaper, Fort Benton Montana, "River Port to Cattle Town Was Easy Transition for Fort Benton," June 9, 1976, pg. 7B
- National Society DAR website, "Old Fort Benton Blockhouse," at https://www.dar.org/national-society/historic-sites-and-properties/old-fort-benton-blockhouse

*Old Fort Benton Blockhouse Doorway, 2018*

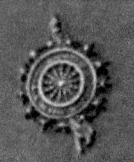

# OLD FORT PECK

OLD FORT PECK WAS LOCATED ABOUT A MILE ABOVE THE PRESENT DAM SITE. BUILT IN 1867 AS A TRADING POST AND AN AGENCY IN 1871, IT SERVED ALSO AS QUARTERS FOR MILITARY AND GOVERNMENT OFFICIALS WHEN NEGOTIATING WITH THE INDIANS. IT WAS ABANDONED IN 1879 DUE TO RIVER EROSION AND THE AGENCY MOVED TO POPLAR.

PLACED BY:
MILK RIVER CHAPTER DAR

*Fort Peck DAR marker (above) and its site (below), 2017*

## 15. OLD FORT PECK

Near town of Fort Peck
GPS coordinates: 48.00166666 | -106.409665028

| | |
|---|---|
| **Commemorates** | Historic Fort Peck, which served as a trading post, military fort, and Indian agency |
| **Site Location** | 2 miles northeast of Fort Peck, 17 miles south of Glasgow, at entrance to Powerhouse Museum |
| **Installed** | May 21, 1970 |
| **Wording** | "Old Fort Peck was located about a mile above the present dam site. Built in 1867 as a trading post and an agency in 1871, it served also as headquarters for military and government officials when negotiating with the Indians. It was abandoned in 1879 due to river erosion and the agency moved to Poplar. Placed by Milk River Chapter DAR" |

## History

It was on May 21, 1970, that the Milk River Chapter, NSDAR placed a marker at historic Fort Peck. The plaque was sited in the entrance to the first powerhouse, which also features a museum. The chapter's intent was to give visitors an opportunity to learn a bit of early history and to preserve the significance of the historic Fort Peck name. Honorary State Regent Mrs. Alexander Torkelson and Milk River Chapter members including Mrs. E.L. Jennings, Mrs. G.R. Austin, Mrs. H.L. Wiley, Mrs. Hyram Peters, and Mrs. Laura Coleman, dedicated the marker.

Old Fort Peck, located about one mile above the present dam site, was built on the west bank of the Missouri River. It was built as a trading post in 1867 by Abel Farwell, a member of the firm of Durfee and Peck (the founders were Colonel Campbell K. Peck, for whom it was named, and Commander E.H. Durfee). The post was constructed of cottonwood log walls 12 feet high, set vertically, and had three bastions and three gateways on the front and two bastions on the rear. It was 300 feet square and contained enclosed quarters for men, store houses, a blacksmith shop, stables, and corrals.

The post was set on a narrow ledge of shale about 35 feet above the river with its rear wall abutting the hillside. A visitor in the 1870s wrote that the front of the stockade was so close to the edge of the ledge that there was barely room to turn around a team and wagon. However the post's location close to the river and its wharf enabled it to serve as a convenient steamboat landing for sternwheelers making trips as far upstream as Fort Benton.

The post soon established a monopoly on fur trade with the Sioux and Assiniboine Indians. To peaceful Indians, it was an important trading post; to trappers and rivermen, it was a safe shelter from warlike Indians. Sternwheel steamers loaded and unloaded there and took on wood for steam for their journeys. Fort Peck became an Indian Agency in 1871 and also served as headquarters for military and government officials when negotiating with Indians. The Fort was abandoned in

July 14, 1879, due to river erosion, and the Indian Agency moved to Poplar. Then, finally, in 1918, the river channel changed and destroyed all traces of the site of Old Fort Peck.

The current Fort Peck Dam Museum tells the history of the construction of the dam and power plants and includes a fossil display of fossils, including a Triceratops skull.

Fort Peck Dam is notable because it is the largest hydraulically filled earth dam in the world, measuring 21,026 feet long and 250.5 feet high, spanning 3.5 miles across the Missouri River from bluff to bluff. Its original purpose was not only to control floods, but also to create jobs during the Depression. In 1933, its construction was the nation's largest public works project, providing 10,456 jobs at its peak. It was completed in 1940.

SOURCES

- Historic monument records, Office of the Historian General, Washington D.C.
- *State Centennial History, MSSDAR*, by Iris McKinney Gray, Vol. V 1894-1994
- *Historical Sites Preserved and Markers Erected by MSSDAR and Its Chapters, 1899-1977*, by Mrs. R.V. Love and Mrs. E.E. Bruno
- *MSSDAR 1982-1984 Pictorial Supplement to Historic Events of 1894-1977*, by Mrs. R.V. Love, Mrs. Sidney Groff and Miss Lorene Burks
- "Old Fort Peck," FortPeckDam.com, at http://www.fortpeckdam.com/historypages/?p=18

*Montana's Real Daughter Orpha Zilpha Parke Bovee grave site (2017)*

# 16. Montana Real Daughter Orpha Zilpha Parke Bovee

Glendive
GPS coordinates: 47.109448 | -104.696795

| | |
|---|---|
| **Commemorates** | Orpha Zilpha Parke Bovee |
| **Site Location** | Dawson County Cemetery, Glendive |
| **Installed** | *Insignia placed*: June 14, 1947 |
| | *Rededication*: June 11, 2011 |
| **Wording** | *Original*: DAR insignia placed on the foot of the gravesite |
| | *Rededication*: "NSDAR Real Daughter Orpha Parke Bovee National No. 87088. Daughter of Ruben Parke Revolutionary War Soldier Connecticut. Marker placed by Montana State Society NSDAR 2011" |

## About "DAR Real Daughters"

All Daughters of the American Revolution are descended from Revolutionary War patriots and soldiers. A surprising number of daughters of America's first patriots were still alive in 1890 when DAR was founded. In fact, 770 women once held the distinction of being called "Real Daughters," who are DAR members just a single generation removed from the Revolutionary War. Many of these women were the youngest daughters of a large family or the result of a marriage late in life.

Not to be confused with the "daughter of a Revolutionary war soldier or patriot," a Real Daughter is distinguished by DAR because she was a DAR member as well as the actual daughter of a soldier or patriot. In the early years of the National Society, a DAR chapter who could name one or more of the 770 Real Daughters among its members was extremely proud of this living link to the American Revolution. Montana has two such Daughters – in addition to Orpha Zilpha Parke Bovee, another Real Daughter is buried in Montana, Caroline Reed Stone (in Shelby). *(See chapter titled "Montana Real Daughter Caroline Reed Stone.")*

## Orpha Zilpha Parke Bovee, a Real Daughter

Mrs. Bovee's gravesite has a bronze DAR insignia at the foot of her gravestone and a DAR plaque above her gravestone, sponsored by the Shining Mountain Chapter, NSDAR of Billings.

Her father, Ruben Parke of Sharon, Connecticut, enlisted as a volunteer soldier in 1781 at the age of 17 years, serving and receiving pay in the Continental Army during the American Revolution from January 1st to December 31st in Captain Douglas' Company, 5th Regulars, Connecticut Lines, New London, Connecticut. Also in 1781, Elizabeth Ford was born in Hartford, Connecticut, and 17 years later married Ruben Parke. Orpha Zilpha's father Ruben died in 1856 at age

92. Her mother, Elizabeth Ford Parke, died in 1876 at the age of 95 years and was buried at DeKalb, Illinois.

Orpha Zilpha, born May 14, 1811, in Ovid Township, New York, was the youngest of six children. She obtained a liberal education for those times and taught school until she was married at the age of 22 to Richard Bovee and moved with him to Indiana. Later Richard and Orpha and their five little girls settled on 320 acres of land 50 miles west of Chicago where he became well-to-do. He died at age 70 and is buried in DeKalb, Illinois.

In 1911, Orpha Zilpha Parke Bovee moved to Montana to live with her daughter, Emily West Bovee (Mrs. Sam) at their ranch home near Cedar, Montana. She died there January 16, 1913, at the age of 101 years, 8 months and 2 days. Her funeral was January 20, 1913, at the Glendive Methodist Episcopal Church, followed by burial in the Dawson County Cemetery.

Mrs. Bovee was not a member of The Montana Society DAR. Her membership was held in Downers Grove, Illinois (#87088). She was accepted by the National Society DAR in June 1911 shortly after the one hundredth anniversary of her birth. Orpha told Downers Grove Chapter members that she remembered her uncle, Captain Almon Ford, and her grandfather, Smith Parke, talking about the Battle of Bunker Hill, in which they both participated.

On June 14, 1947, a bronze DAR insignia was placed on Mrs. Bovee's gravestone by the Yellowstone River Chapter, NSDAR (now overseen by the Shining Mountain Chapter). During World War II, Shining Mountain Chapter had begun the process of obtaining a Real Daughter marker for Mrs. Bovee's grave. But the Government Copper Conservation Order, which prohibited the use of bronze and other strategic metals, cancelled the order for the marker. Finally, in 1947, the marker was cast and placed on Mrs. Bovee's grave. The 1947 marker dedication was held at 1:30 in the afternoon and featured remarks by former State Regent Mrs. C.A. Rasmusson, and Shining Mountain Chapter Chair of Ceremonies Mrs. A.T. Nelson and Regent Mrs. M.B. Yates.

Most recently, on June 11, 2011, then-State Regent Peggy Salitros led the dedication of a bronze plaque placed at the top of Mrs. Bovee's gravesite to honor the 200$^{th}$ anniversary of her 1811 birth. This recognition came from a project of former State Regent JoAnn Piazzola to ensure that all Real Daughter graves in Montana were appropriately marked. The dedication ceremony drew DAR members from across Montana, along with Dawson County Commissioner Skillstad and Mayor Jerry Jimison.

**SOURCES**

- *Record of Tablets and Markers Placed by Montana DAR 1908-1947*, by Mrs. Fred E. May
- *State Centennial History, MSSDAR*, by Iris McKinney Gray, Vol. V 1894-1994
- *Historical Sites Preserved and Markers Erected by MSSDAR and Its Chapters 1899-1977*, by Mrs. R.V. Love and Mrs. E.E. Bruno
- *MSSDAR 1982-1984 Pictorial Supplement to Historic Events of 1894-1977*, by Mrs. R.V. Love, Mrs. Sidney Groff and Miss Lorene Burks
- *Yellowstone Monitor* newspaper, Glendive Montana, "Last of 'Real Daughters of the Revolution' is Gone," Jan. 23, 1913
- *DAR American Spirit Magazine*, "Born to Greatness: The Daughters of the First Patriots," Sept./Oct 2007
- MSSDAR Big Sky Banner newsletter, July 2011, pg. 1

*Orpha Zilpha Parke Bovee grave site (2017)*

*Giant Springs DAR marker, 2017*

# 17. GIANT SPRINGS

Six miles northeast of Great Falls
GPS coordinates: 47.5339 | -111.2299

| | |
|---|---|
| **Commemorates** | Discovery of Giant Fountain by Captain Clark, June 18, 1805 |
| **Site Location** | Giant Springs State Park (off Highway 87, 1 mile east on River Dr. to Giant Springs Rd.) |
| **Installed** | May 30, 1928 |
| **Wording** | "Lewis and Clark on their historic expedition to the Pacific Coast discovered this giant fountain June 18-1805. In honor of the courage, fidelity and patriotism of the explorers this tablet is here placed and dedicated by Black Eagle Chapter Daughters of the American Revolution Great Falls, Montana May 30-1928" |

## HISTORY

This DAR marker, consisting of a bronze tablet sized 26 by 30 inches inset to a six-ton boulder set on a concrete base, was dedicated on Memorial Day 1928 by Black Eagle, NSDAR Chapter. The bronze tablet was given by the Anaconda Copper Mining Company and placed on the boulder by the firm Grover & Leuchars of Great Falls. The large granite six-ton boulder, donated by Ralph Budd, president of the Great Northern Railway, was brought to Great Falls from Elk Park, 150 miles away. The concrete base for the marker was equally substantial–it was reported to be three feet deep, four feet long, and six feet wide. The Montana Power Company hauled the boulder to Great Falls and placed it on a concrete base that they specially made for the marker.

A crowd of 1,000 witnessed the dedication. Black Eagle Chapter Regent Mrs. O.B. Nelson formally presented the marker after it was unveiled by Shirley Case Abrams, a descendant of a Revolutionary War soldier. Other dignitaries included Montana's Lieutenant Governor W.S. McCormack (Kalispell), who accepted the monument on behalf of the state, Mayor H.B. Mitchell, who accepted the monument on behalf of the city of Great Falls, and Montana State Historical Society librarian David Hilger, who accepted the monument on behalf of the Historical Society.

Master of Ceremonies and chair of the DAR Marker Committee, Mrs. George H. Berry, said in her address to the crowd:

> *The Committee decided that there should be no drive put on for the raising of funds, but the matter was laid before the Montana Power Company, the Great Northern Railway, and the Anaconda Copper Mining Company with the result that the plan was carried out… Thus we come to you today with our task completed, feeling that we have placed a monument here that will stand for all time to come and one that will be a reminder to those who come after us of the heroic deeds and the sacrifices made by these early explorers.*

Other members of the Marker Committee were Regent Mrs. O.B. Nelson, Mrs. C.A. McKinney and Mrs. Jack Abrams.

This springs, originally called a fountain, was fan shaped and between 300 and 400 feet wide. It is now known as Giant Springs. Currently flowing at 156 million gallons of water per day, its water is a constant 54 degrees and has been dated using chlorofluorocarbons (CFCs) to be about 25 years old. The springs' origin is high in the Little Belt Mountains, 40 miles to the south, where rainfall and snow melt filter through the 250 million year old Madison Limestone Formation. Giant Springs feeds the Roe River, which was once registered by the *Guinness Book of World Records* as the shortest river in the world; it is about 200 feet long. (Guinness no longer lists Shortest River in the World as a category.) The Roe flows immediately into the Missouri River.

Captain Clark and five of his men discovered the giant pool on the south bank of the Missouri River between Rainbow and Black Eagle Falls. They reported that they "proceeded on up the river a little more than a mile to the largest fountain or Spring I ever Saw, and doubt if it is not the largest in American Known." It was here that the Expedition spent more time than at any other point on their westward journey.

## Sources
- Historic monument records, Office of the Historian General, Washington D.C.
- *Record of Tablets and Markers Placed by Montana DAR 1908-1947*, by Mrs. Fred E. May
- *State Centennial History, MSSDAR*, by Iris McKinney Gray, Vol. V 1894-1994
- *Historical Sites Preserved and Markers Erected by MSSDAR and Its Chapters 1899-1977*, by Mrs. R.V. Love and Mrs. E.E. Bruno
- *MSSDAR 1982-1984 Pictorial Supplement to Historic Events of 1894-1977*, by Mrs. R.V. Love, Mrs. Sidney Groff and Miss Lorene Burks
- *The River Press* newspaper, Fort Benton Montana, "Daughters of American Revolution Unveil Monument to Lewis and Clark," July 11, 1928
- Assistance with historic facts by John Taillie, Region 4 Parks Manager and Clark Carlson-Thompson, Park Manager, Giant Springs and Ackley Lake State Parks, Montana Fish, Wildlife and Parks

*Veterans Memorial Tree DAR marker (above) and site (below), 2015*

# 18. VETERANS MEMORIAL TREE

Great Falls
GPS coordinates: 47.517364 | -111.261950

| | |
|---|---|
| **Commemorates** | Montana's largest veterans memorial |
| **Site Location** | Veterans Memorial Park, in north Great Falls (1025 25th Street North) |
| **Installed** | September 28, 2006 |
| **Wording** | "Gift of Black Eagle-Assinniboine Chapter Daughters of the American Revolution" |

## HISTORY

This black granite DAR marker was dedicated at 4:00 p.m. on September 28, 2006, shortly after its companion donation, a flowering crabapple tree, was planted. Black Eagle Assinniboine Chapter Regent Anna Beckman Weaver led DAR's effort to place a tree to shade visitors, especially those attending Memorial Day ceremonies there.

The Montana Veterans Memorial overlooks the Missouri River. Dedicated on Memorial Day 2006 (May 29), it is the largest memorial to veterans in Montana. It was built to honor all who served in all branches of the United States armed forces, in peace and in war.

The memorial was designed by Great Falls architect Gene Davidson and largely built on volunteer labor. The local paper reported that "The Red Horse Squad at Malmstrom and a Montana Seabees Unit together contributed about $450,000 in volunteer labor."

The Veterans Memorial is unique in that it makes a special effort to honor Blackfeet Indians for whom around 200 tiles have been installed to date. (Native Americans serve in the military at greater rates than the national average, notably so for Montana's Indian tribes.)

It is said that when General John Jay Pershing was stationed at Fort Assinniboine near Havre, he bivouacked on the memorial's site.

**Sources**

- *Montana Senior News*, "A Fitting Tribute to Those Who've Served: The Montana Veterans Memorial in Great Falls," Oct. 1, 2018
- *The Great Falls Tribune* newspaper, "Veterans Memorial Celebrates 10th Birthday," May 22, 2016

*Old postmarks—Fort Custer 1895 (above) and Fort Logan 1909 (below)*

*Fort Custer plaque (above) and marker at site (below), 2017*

# 19. Fort Custer

Hardin

GPS coordinates: 45.739129 | -107.586995

| | |
|---|---|
| **Commemorates** | Site of Fort Custer, named after General George Armstrong Custer |
| **Site Location** | *Original:* Original fort location |
| | *Current:* Big Horn County Historical Museum parking lot |
| **Installed** | September 21, 1930 |
| **Wording** | "Fort Custer - Established as a military post November 1877 by order of President Rutherford B. Hayes and General Phil H. Sheridan. Garrisoned as one of the important Military posts in the Northwest until abandoned by the Government, September 1897. This Fort was named in honor of General George A. Custer, who was killed in action with his entire command at the Battle of Little Big Horn, June 25, 1876. Dedicated by Shining Mountain Daughters of the American Revolution, Billings, Montana September 21, 1930" |

# History

On September 21, 1930, Shining Mountain Chapter, NSDAR, aided by the Lions Club and Commercial Club of Hardin, erected and dedicated a bronze tablet mounted on a granite boulder at Fort Custer. The tablet was donated by the Anaconda Copper Mining Company.

Fort Custer, established in June 1877 by order of President Rutherford B. Hayes, was under the military direction of Army General Phil H. Sheridan. Construction of the fort was led by Lieutenant Colonel G.P. Buell of the 11th Infantry who arrived on the steamer Florence Meyer. His command of four companies and a large force of mechanics and laborers built the fort entirely of native materials such as cottonwood and bricks made on site. When complete, Fort Custer had quarters for 10 companies, including stables for six cavalry troops, but had no walls or other fortifications. It was built on a bluff overlooking the confluence of the Big Horn and the Little Big Horn Rivers.

After its temporary name of Big Horn Post, on November 8, 1877, the fort was named for General George Armstrong Custer, who was killed with his entire command at the Battle of the Little Big Horn.

In its day, Fort Custer was one of the best-equipped and largest cavalry posts in the country and for many years was the headquarters of the 2nd U.S. Cavalry. Many young officers who served there later went on to high ranks. Among these are Major General Hugh L. Scott (Chief of Staff of the U.S. Army), Major General Hunter Liggett (commander of the first American Army in France in World War I), Brigadier General David L. Brainard (one of two survivors of the famous Greely Artic expedition), and Rear Admiral Frank P. Upham (the only Naval cadet from Montana to reach that rank; as a boy, he played at Fort Custer where his father was a 1st U.S. Cavalry Captain).

By the time the fort was established, most hostile Indians in the vicinity had been confined to reservations, but the post did supply troops for some Plains campaigns, including the 1878 Bannock War and an 1877 uprising at the Crow Agency. In 1886, when Yellowstone National Park asked the U.S. Army for help policing the Park, Fort Custer soldiers began what would be over 30 years of military presence in the Park. The fort closed April 17, 1898, and the buildings sold off.

In 1930 when the DAR marker was originally placed, it stood on a well-traveled road at the edge of the fort grounds. Later, the Big Horn County Historical Museum contacted Shining Mountain Chapter about relocating the marker to the grounds of the museum in Hardin because it could no longer be accessed (it was then located on private property). Additionally, the marker had suffered damage from bullets.

In 2016, the marker in its entirety was moved to the museum's parking lot. From where it now sits, when looking up at the bluffs in the distance, is Fort Custer's original location.

SOURCES
- Historic monument records, Office of the Historian General, Wash. D.C.
- *Record of Tablets and Markers Placed by Montana DAR 1908-1947*, by Mrs. Fred E. May
- *State Centennial History, MSSDAR*, by Iris McKinney Gray, 1894-1994
- *Historical Sites Preserved and Markers Erected by MSSDAR and Its Chapters 1899-1977*, by Mrs. R.V. Love and Mrs. E.E. Bruno
- *MSSDAR 1982-1984 Pictorial Supplement to Historic Events of 1894-1977*, by Mrs. R.V. Love, Mrs. Sidney Groff and Miss Lorene Burks
- "War Department. Fort Custer, Montana. 11/8/1877-4/17/1898 Organization Authority Record," National Archives Catalog at https://catalog.archives.gov/id/10454804
- *Big Timber Pioneer* newspaper, Big Timber Montana, "D.A.R. Will Mark Site of Fort Custer," Sept. 4, 1930

*Rosebud "Battleground" site (above) and monument (below), 2017*

# 20. Rosebud Battlefield

40 miles southeast of Hardin
GPS coordinates: 45.219714 | -106.949397

| | |
|---|---|
| **Commemorates** | U.S. soldiers killed June 17, 1876, when General Crook engaged Indian Tribes under Crazy Horse |
| **Site Location** | Along Rosebud Creek in Big Horn County off MT-314; a Montana State Park and a National Historic Landmark |
| **Installed** | June 17, 1934 |
| **Wording** | "In grateful recognition of the valor and sacrifice of the soldiers killed in an action fought on these grounds, between the United States Forces under General George Crook and Sioux and Cheyenne Indians under Chief Crazy Horse. June 17, 1876. 3$^{rd}$ U.S. Cavalry |

Sergt. David Marshall    Pvt. Brooks Conner
Sergt. Anton Neukirchen   Pvt. Eugene Flynn
Pvt. William W. Allen    Pvt. Allen J. Mitchell
Pvt. Richard W. Bennett   Pvt. George Potts
Pvt. Gilbert Roe

Erected by Shining Mountain Chapter Daughters of the American Revolution, Billings and citizens of Rosebud and Big Horn Counties, Montana. Dedicated June 17, 1934"

# History

On June 17, 1934, at 2:00 in the afternoon, Shining Mountain Chapter, NSDAR dedicated a monument of concrete and cinder stones gathered from the Rosebud battlefield to honor the U.S. troops who died there on June 17, 1876. The Anaconda Copper Mining Company donated the bronze plaque, made of native Montana ore.

At the unveiling and dedication ceremony, John Arnold, member of the Montana House of Representatives from Rosebud County, began with a call to order. Next, Mrs. R.C. Dilavou of Billings, DAR state regent, presided over the ceremony. Ben Harwood, a Billings attorney, gave the main address, and State DAR Chair of Markers, Mrs. C.A. Rasmusson of Helena officially presented the bronze tablet to Robert Vickers, newspaper publisher at Hardin. The ceremony included government and state officials as well as many other prominent men and women. Among those present were a number of Cheyenne Indians, including four aged warriors who took part in the battle–Beaver Heart, Louis Dog, Charles Limpy and Wheezer Bear.

The six-hour battle took place only eight days before the defeat of General Custer and his entire command at the Battle of the Little Big Horn. It was one of the largest battles of the Indian wars. Brigadier General George Crook led his 1,050 troops and 260 Crow and Shoshone scouts against a similar number of Indians, led by Sioux Chief Crazy Horse and Cheyenne Chiefs Two Moon, Young Two Moon, and Spotted Wolf. The battle was a confused one, held over uneven ground in three pitched skirmishes. There were numerous brave acts on both sides, including a Cheyenne girl, Buffalo Calf Road

Woman, who rescued her brother, Chief Comes-In-Sight, after his horse was shot out from under him. (In fact, the battle is known by the Northern Cheyenne as "Where the Girl Saved Her Brother.")

Nine soldiers were killed in action, and Crazy Horse lost 13 warriors. Although Crook claimed the battle as a victory due to routing the Indians, he withdrew his troops to recuperate, providing fewer men in the later fight at the Battle of the Little Big Horn.

The Rosebud Battlefield was added to the National Register of Historic Places partially due to the efforts of Elmer E. "Slim" Kobold who homesteaded the battlefield area. He refused to allow mining of a rich coal seam under his ranch in an effort to preserve this historic location for future generations. In 1978, the site became a Montana State Park, purchased largely from the state's Coal Tax Fund.

*(**A note on terminology**: this site has changed in official designation from "battleground" to "battlefield.")*

### Sources

- Historic monument records, Office of the Historian General, Wash. D.C.
- *Record of Tablets and Markers Placed by Montana DAR 1908-1947*, by Mrs. Fred E. May
- *State Centennial History, MSSDAR*, by Iris McKinney Gray, Vol. V 1894-1994
- *Historical Sites Preserved and Markers Erected by MSSDAR and Its Chapters 1899-1977*, by Mrs. R.V. Love and Mrs. E.E. Bruno
- *MSSDAR 1982-1984 Pictorial Supplement to Historic Events of 1894-1977*, by Mrs. R.V. Love, Mrs. Sidney Groff and Miss Lorene Burks
- "Battle of the Rosebud," http://www.u-s-history.com/pages/h1382.html
- *The Billings Gazette* newspaper, Billings Montana, "Site of Battle of the Rosebud Between Sioux And Crook's Forces Will Be Marked on Sunday, Billings DAR Chapter Will place Tablet at Ceremonies," June 10, 1934
- *The Billings Gazette* newspaper, Billings Montana, "Wrinkled Cheyenne Warriors Tell of Battle With Crook and His Soldiers on the Rosebud," June 24, 1934

*Bear Paw "Battleground" DAR marker - side 1, 2017*

## 21. Bear Paw Battlefield

16 miles south of Chinook
GPS coordinates: 48.377982| -109.212070

| | |
|---|---|
| **Commemorates** | Nez Perce Flight of 1877 |
| **Site Location** | A National Historic Park and part of the Nez Perce National Historic Trail, administered by the U.S. Forest Service |
| **Installed** | September 30, 1929 |
| **Wording** | *East-facing tablet*: "Bear's Paw Battleground. Commemorating the surrender of Chief Joseph and the remnant of his tribe of Nez Perces to General Nelson A. Miles, October 5, 1877. Here Chiefs Looking Glass, Ollicut, Too-Hul-Hul-Sote and many other warriors were killed. Chief Joseph was a military genius, courageous and humane. Presenting his rifle to General Mills, with right hand upraised, he proclaimed: 'From where the sun now stands, I will fight no more forever.' He kept his word. Dedicated by the Daughters of the American Revolution and the citizens of Blaine County, Montana, September 30, 1929" |

*West-facing tablet*: "Bear's Paw Battleground. In grateful remembrance of the officers and enlisted men killed in action in the last decisive armed conflict between the white men and red men in the Northwest. September 30-October 5, 1877.

7th U.S. Cavalry

Captain Owen Hale
2nd Lieut. Jonathan W. Biddle
1st Sergt. George McDermott
1st Sergt. Michael Martin
1st Sergt. Otto Wild
Sergt. James H. Alberts
Sergt. Otto Durselow
Sergt. Max Mielke
Sergt. Henry W. Raichel
Pvt. John E. Cleveland
Pvt. David I. Dawsey
Pvt. Charles F. Hurdick
Pvt. Frank Knaupp
Pvt. Lewis Kelly
Pvt. Samuel McIntyre
Pvt. William J. Randall
Pvt. Francis Roth
Pvt. William Whitlow

2nd U.S. Cavalry

Pvt. John Irving

5th U.S. Cavalry

Corporal John Haddo
Pvt. Thomas Ceoghegan
Pvt. Joseph KohlerPvt. Richard M. Peshall

Erected by the Daughters of the American Revolution and the Citizens of Blaine County, Montana. September 30, 1929"

# HISTORY

The DAR Markers Committee of the Montana State Society erected two markers at the Battle of Bear Paw site near Chinook in Blaine County. The bronze tablets, given by the Anaconda Copper Mining Company, were set into and made part of a seven-foot tall monument constructed of concrete and boulders gathered from the old battlefield. When first installed, the tablets faced both east and west.

The west-facing tablet tells that the monument is in remembrance of officers and enlisted men of the U.S. Army killed in action and gives their names–twenty-three in all. The east-facing bronze tablet commemorates the surrender of Chief Joseph and his tribe of Nez Perce to General Nelson A. Miles October 5, 1877.

On the Snake Creek battlefield in the foothills of the Bears Paw Mountains south of Chinook, a band of Nez Perce Indians under Chief Joseph and the army under General Nelson A. Miles fought from September 30 to October 5, 1877. It was the last battle of the Indian Wars in the Northwest. This brought to an end the gallant actions of Chief Joseph and his band of approximately 800 Nez Perce who refused to recognize the land sessions made to the U.S. by the Treaty of 1863.

Chief Joseph was a strong defender of his people's rights, and feeling that they could not obtain justice in the United States, in 1877 he determined to lead them from their homeland in central Idaho into Canada. Accordingly, he set out on a hard march of 1,170 miles with 800 Nez Perce among whom were only around 200 warriors. The rest were women, children and old men. On this retreat, Chief Joseph and his warriors stunned the U.S. by defeating them in skirmishes where the Indians were greatly outnumbered. The first day of the battle at Snake Creek in the Bears Paw Mountains, September 30, 1877, the U.S. troops lost nearly twenty percent of their force to the small band of Nez Perce.

At Snake Creek, 40 miles from their goal of the Canadian border, this courageous little band was so greatly out-numbered that they were forced to surrender. They had lost their horses, their food supply was cut off, and during the battle many of their greatest warriors were killed. It was here that Chief Joseph made his famous statement:

*I am tired of fighting. Our chiefs are killed. Looking Glass is dead. Tulhuulhulsuit is dead. The old men are all dead. It is the young men who say, 'Yes' or 'No.' He who led the young men is dead. It is cold, and we have no blankets. The little children are freezing to death. My people, some of them, have run away to the hills, and have no blankets, no food. No one knows where they are, perhaps freezing to death. I want to have time to look for my children, and see how many of them I can find. Maybe I shall find them among the dead. Hear me, my chiefs. I am tired. My heart is sick and sad. From where the sun now stands, I will fight no more forever.*

Notably, Chief Joseph has the distinction of being only one of two Nez Perce leaders to survive; the other, White Bird, reached Canada with 200 to 300 Nez Perce. In fact, Chief Joseph was a leader of just one of the five bands of non-treaty Nez Perce.

After his surrender, Chief Joseph was taken to Fort Leavenworth, Kansas, but his exile from his homeland continued at the Colville Indian Reservation near Spokane, Washington. From there, he spent the rest of his life working diligently for the benefit of his people—even making a trip to Washington, D.C. on their behalf. He died in 1904.

(***A note on terminology***: *this site has changed in official designation from "battleground" to "battlefield."*)

### Sources

- *Record of Tablets and Markers Placed by Montana DAR 1908-1947*, by Mrs. Fred E. May
- *Historical Sites Preserved and Markers Erected by MSSDAR and Its Chapters 1899-1977*, by Mrs. R.V. Love and Mrs. E.E. Bruno
- *MSSDAR 1982-1984 Pictorial Supplement to Historic Events of 1894-1977*, by Mrs. R.V. Love, Mrs. Sidney Groff and Miss Lorene Burks
- *The River Press* newspaper, Fort Benton Montana, "Gen. Scott to be at Chinook," Sept. 25, 1920
- *The Mineral Independent* newspaper, Superior Montana, October 3, 1929

- *The Montana Standard* newspaper, Butte Montana, "Chief Joseph Battlefield Ranger's Lifelong Obsession," July 20, 1997, pg. 15
- National Park Service, Bear Paw Battlefield History at https://www.nps.gov/nepe/learn/historyculture/bear-paw-battlefield-history.htm

*Bear Paw "Battleground" DAR marker – side 2, 2017*

*Fort Assiniboine DAR marker (above) and marker site (below), 2017*

## 22. FORT ASSINNIBOINE

6 miles south of Havre
GPS coordinates: 48.498611 | -109.796464

| | |
|---|---|
| **Commemorates** | 2nd largest military post in the U.S. in 1878 |
| **Site Location** | South of Havre on Highway 87 |
| **Installed** | November 2, 1958 |
| **Wording** | "Fort Assiniboine, Guardian of Montana's Frontier, was established by Act of Congress in May, 1878. Lt. Colonel Brooks selected this high site on Beaver Creek and superintended the million-dollar construction of the fort, which took its name from the neighboring Assiniboine Indian tribe. The infantry and cavalry detachments stationed here to hold off marauding Indians, including Sitting Bull's hostile Sioux, never actually took part in a single engagement after Fort Assiniboine was completed, but this new post became one of four important forts nominally guarding the border. General Pershing, then a young lieutenant, served here in the 'nineties.' After the Tenth Cavalry was ordered to Cuba in 1898, Fort Assiniboine was practically abandoned; and in 1911 President Taft signed the bill which abolished the largest military reservation in the United States." |

# History

The Assinniboine Chapter, NSDAR placed and dedicated a marker of cement and stone on the grounds at Fort Assiniboine. According to an account of the project in *Historic Events*, K. Ross Toole of the Montana Historical Society worked with Mrs. Max Kuhr and Mrs. Earl Clack to compose "the true legend of Fort Assiniboine" as told on the bronze DAR marker. The Anaconda Copper Mining Company contributed the copper plaque and inscribed it. The plaque was set in an upright block of granite which had been one of the foundation stones of the old water tower at the fort and is "enhanced by a graceful wall of native Montana stone and a cantilevered concrete seat."

On December 30, 1878, the 220,000-acre site was dubbed Fort Assiniboine, with one "n"; the fort retained that spelling until officially changed to Fort Assinniboine on December 3, 1884. The fort was one of just a few open-planned post (fort) complexes constructed between 1877 and 1879 in Montana, the Dakotas, Wyoming, Nebraska, and Idaho. It was mainly for border patrol and engagement with the Cree, Metis, Blackfeet Indians, and Sioux Indians, but its location between the Blackfeet reservation to the west and Fort Belknap to the east led to interaction with the Gros Ventre and Assiniboine Indians as well. The fort's role in the United States military and diplomatic relationships with tribes and Canada was important, as the mere fact of its existence likely dissuaded actions by Indian nations. Because Fort Assinniboine's personnel were charged not only with protection and assistance, they also were responsible for patrol, seizure, deportation, and combat. In so doing, they influenced national Indian policy and impacted the lifeways of nearby native populations.

Over its 32 years as a military post, the fort garrisoned hundreds of soldiers, including African-American companies from the 24th and 25th Infantries and 10th U.S. Cavalry (the famed "Buffalo Soldiers").

In 1903, Congress designated Fort Assinniboine a training facility and invested in new construction and renovations. However, because of the fort's remoteness and harsh winters, combined with shifts in military priorities, its training role diminished until 1911, when the military abandoned the fort and transferred it to the Interior Department. After 1913, part of the property transitioned to state ownership as an agricultural experiment station and a large part was for Rocky Boy's Reservation; some land became Beaver Creek Park.

In a November 29, 1941 letter to the Assinniboine Chapter, General John J. Pershing extended greetings and good wishes. He had learned that the fort was the theme of the 39th annual DAR conference in Havre and recalled that he served at the fort 50 years prior.

This site is listed on the National Register of Historic Places and is part of the Old Forts Trail, an international heritage tourism trail connecting seven historic forts in Montana, Alberta, and Saskatchewan.

*(**Spelling note**: The generally-accepted spelling of the Indian tribe is "Assiniboins"; the DAR chapter's name is spelled "Assinniboine"; and the Fort name began as "Assiniboine" but was later changed to "Assinniboine.")*

### SOURCES

- Historic monument records, Office of the Historian General, Wash. DC
- *State Centennial History, MSSDAR*, by Iris McKinney Gray, 1894-1994
- *Historical Sites Preserved and Markers Erected by MSSDAR and Its Chapters 1899-1977*, by Mrs. R.V. Love and Mrs. E.E. Bruno
- *MSSDAR 1982-1984 Pictorial Supplement to Historic Events of 1894-1977*, by Mrs. R.V. Love, Mrs. Sidney Groff and Miss Lorene Burks
- Archives West, Fort Assinniboine records, 1879-1906 at http://archiveswest.orbiscascade.org/ark:/80444/xv24629

*Gates of the Mountains marker (above) and site (below), 2017*

# 23. Gates of The Mountains

North of Helena
GPS coordinates: 46.8705 | -111.9023

| | |
|---|---|
| **Commemorates** | Lewis and Clark's exploration of Meriwether Canyon and their July 19, 1805, campsite near there |
| **Site Location** | 20 miles north of Helena, off I-15, Meriwether Picnic Area of the Gates of the Mountains Wilderness, accessible via boat trip; marker moved in 1951 and again in the late 1970s |
| **Installed** | *Original:* July 19, 1927 |
| | *Rededicated*: July 26, 1945 |
| **Wording** | "In commemoration of the intrepid explorers, comprising the Lewis and Clark Expedition who discovered this canyon and encamped here July 19-1805 on their westward voyage of trans-continental exploration enroute up the Missouri River bound for the Pacific Northwest. Dedicated by Oro Fino Chapter Daughters of the American Revolution, July 19, 1927" |

# History

The Oro Fino Chapter, NSDAR dedicated a 24-by-36 inch bronze plaque, donated by the Anaconda Copper Mining Company, on the 122$^{nd}$ anniversary of the Lewis and Clark Expedition's making camp at the site. Over 200 people attended the event, including Governor John E. Erickson (who accepted the monument on behalf of the state of Montana), Chief Justice L.L. Callaway, Congressman Scott Leavitt, Montana State Regent Mrs. C.A. Rasmusson, Oro Fino Chapter Regent Mrs. M.A. Brannon, and State Historian David Hilger (who accepted the marker on behalf of the State Historical Society).

It was on July 19, 1805, with Captain Meriwether Lewis in command of 29 men, that the campsite was made. Among the party was Sacajawea, daughter of the Shoshones, who became the guide and inspiration of the party and who within a few days travel from this point, gave invaluable aid and information to those in command when the three forks of the Missouri had been reached.

When Captain Lewis entered the canyon, he noted it contains "the most remarkable clifts that we have yet seen." He wrote in his journals that the cliffs seemed to rise "from the water's edge on either side perpendicularly to the hight of 1200 feet...the tow[er]ing and projecting rocks in many places seem ready to tumble on us." The canyon was dark, especially since they entered it in late afternoon, and the men were forced to continue until after dark before finding a place on the bank with enough room and firewood for the night's camp.

Captain Lewis named the place "gates of the rocky mountains" since it seemed to him that the river appeared to have "forced it's way through this immence body of solid rock for the distance of 5¾ miles."

Captain Clark never saw the Gates of the Mountains. A day earlier (July 18), he and three men detoured by foot over the Prickly Pear Valley, and rejoined the main party after a difficult three-day march.

The 1927 DAR marker was somewhat difficult to find as it was accessible only via boat trip. As described in the *Anaconda Standard* newspaper:

> *The monument stands in about the center of the slightly sloping park at the entrance to the small-bore canyon, about 30 yards from the water-line. It faces the river and is of concrete, five feet six inches high by five feet wide and three feet thick. It rests on a slightly projecting concrete base.*

On July 26, 1945, the DAR marker was rededicated as part of a statewide commemoration of the Lewis and Clark Expedition. The ceremony was held by the Lewis and Clark Chapter of the American Pioneer Trails Association and the Gates of the Mountains Boat Club, who committed to rededicate themselves and their efforts "to the preservation of the canyon's beauty, its interest, and its accessibility for the good of all our people."

In 1951, the DAR marker was relocated to a spot next to the Mann Gulch memorial plaque on a limestone outcrop at the mouth of Meriwether Canyon. (The bronze Mann Gulch memorial sculpture and marker honors 13 smokejumpers who died fighting the 1949 Mann Gulch forest fire.) The two markers are at a public dock on the Missouri River near Mann Gulch.

In the late 1970s, both the DAR bronze plaque and the Mann Gulch sculpture and plaque were moved a few feet higher on the same rock outcrop when a new trail was constructed to improve visitors' views of the markers.

The Montana State Society DAR petitioned its national headquarters in August of 1998 to replace the 1927 marker, which contains some historical inaccuracies. In the end, the marker was not replaced, but if it were, it would have replaced the words "who discovered this canyon" with the more correct "who entered this canyon" and it would have replaced the phrase "encamped here" with "camped near this spot [some distance] to the southwest."

**SOURCES**

- Historic monument records, Office of the Historian General, Washington D.C.
- *Record of Tablets and Markers Placed by Montana DAR 1908-1947*, by Mrs. Fred E. May
- *State Centennial History, MSSDAR*, by Iris McKinney Gray, Vol. V 1894-1994
- *Historical Sites Preserved and Markers Erected by MSSDAR and Its Chapters, 1899-1977*, by Mrs. R.V. Love and Mrs. E.E. Bruno
- *MSSDAR 1982-1984 Pictorial Supplement to Historic Events of 1894-1977*, by Mrs. R.V. Love, Mrs. Sidney Groff and Miss Lorene Burks
- *American Monthly Magazine* (DAR), Sept. 1909, pps. 798-801
- *The Anaconda Standard* newspaper, Anaconda Montana, "Historic Spot in Montana is Marked by Daughters of the American Revolution," July 24, 1927, pg. 20
- *Choteau Acantha* newspaper, Choteau Montana, "Gates of Mountains Discovery is Commemorated by D.A.R. Tablet," Aug. 4, 1927
- *Great Falls Tribune* newspaper, Great Falls Montana, "Lewis, Clark Trip Important to U.S.," July 27, 1945, pg. 1
- *Great Falls Tribune* newspaper, Great Falls Montana, "Forest Service Plans New Wilderness Area," June 2, 1946, pg. 17
- *The Independent-Record* newspaper, Helena Montana, "Memorial Plaque Marks Site of Mann Gulch Fire," June 13, 1951, pg. 3
- *Helena Independent Record* newspaper, Helena Montana, "A Place of Singular Appearance?", May 1, 1997, pg. 6
- Letter from Historian General Mrs. Joseph Linn Colburn, Aug. 28, 1998 to Miss Darlene R. Gilchrist, Regent of Oro Fino Chapter

*State Historian David Hilger, Governor John E. Erickson, State Regent Mrs. C.A. Rasmusson, and others at 1927 dedication of the DAR marker at Meriwether picnic grounds. Printed with permission of the Montana Historical Society Research Center 957-646*

*Reed and Bowles Stockade Trading Post marker, 2015*

# 24. Reed and Bowles Stockade Trading Post

Lewistown
GPS coordinates: 48.377982 | -109.212070

| | |
|---|---|
| **Commemorates** | Historic stockade and trading post on the Carroll Trail |
| **Site Location** | 2 miles north of Lewistown on Poor Farm Loop, a National Register of Historic Places site |
| **Installed** | September 17, 1940 |
| **Wording** | "Location and remnant of Reed and Bowles Stockade, Trading Post and Station on Carroll Trail 1875-1880. Dedicated by Julia Hancock Chapter, Daughters of Am. Rev. September 17, 1940." |

## History

Currently (2019), this site is in the process of archaeologic study and a planned future reconstruction by the Central Montana Historical Society.

In 1940, the Julia Hancock Chapter, NSDAR placed a commemorative historical marker on the north side of the Reed and Bowles Stockade cabin. The marker, 90 pounds of solid Montana metal, was donated by the Anaconda Copper Mining Company.

Constructed in 1875 from logs taken from abandoned Fort Sherman, which was built in 1873, the stockade started as cabin with a gable roof, dirt floor, and 13-high square hewn logs held together with pegs instead of nails. The building was enclosed in a stockade built by standing poles on end in a trench joined close together forming a high fence around a quadrangle about 100 by 150 feet.

By spring of 1875, business partners Alonzo S. Reed and John J. Bowles positioned their Reed and Bowles Trading Post near the Carroll Crossing, where the Carroll Trail crossed Big Spring Creek, to take advantage of what they hoped would be brisk traffic from the anticipated Carroll Trail. They also located the post to be further distant from the newly-established Camp Lewis, a summer camp for Company F of the 7th Infantry which had been tasked with guarding travelers on the Carroll Trail, a freighting route connecting Carroll on the Missouri River and Helena. Reed and Bowles wanted to be away from the watchful eye of the military so they could carry on with their lucrative, but illegal, trade of liquor and firearms with passing Indian tribes. According to historian Brian Schofield:

> *Most of their income was derived from flagrantly ignoring the laws against serving whiskey to Indians—there were rarely any troops posted at nearby Camp Lewis, so the pair were over a hundred miles from justice in all directions—and they lubricated hunting parties with a noxious homebrew reputedly made from ethanol, tobacco, and red pepper.*

In the summers of 1874 and 1875, low water on the Missouri River temporarily made Carroll an attractive port, but freighters soon discovered that the Carroll Road was actually more difficult to travel than the Fort Benton Road to Helena due to the gumbo-mud road. In addition, Lakota Sioux warriors took advantage of the feeble protection provided by over-stretched infantry troops along the route, with bloodshed and horse-stealing a growing occurrence.

Then in 1876, high water allowed most steamboats to continue to Fort Benton's better port facilities and the Carroll Trail was left completely unprotected when most troops were called to the Great Sioux War in southeastern Montana. Thus, the Carroll Trail was a failure. Except for local traffic, freighting along it never revived and the trail was abandoned and later was washed away by Missouri River flooding.

During the 1877 Nez Perce Indians' flight to Canada, Chief Joseph and his followers camped near the Reed and Bowles Stockade shortly before their defeat at the Battle of the Bear Paw.

Despite the failure of the Carroll Trail, Reed and Bowles remained, running a brisk business trading with passing tribes, hunters, and trappers until 1880. The cabin was the last structure remaining of the trading post; the stockade and other cabins no longer remain. According to a 1931 historical account by O.O. Mueller, "In 1883, the original log cabin was enlarged and a new roof put on and since then there have been no changes in the structure except repair to the roof."

History shows Alonzo Reed and John Bowles to be unsavory characters. They arrived in Montana Territory in the 1860s from either Wyoming or Colorado. References to them in Montana begin at Diamond City, the mining camp in Confederate Gulch on the north side of the Helena Valley. Bowles was reportedly a mule skinner assigned to assist soldiers establish Fort Baker in the vicinity, while Reed is first known to have been in company with James M. Cavanaugh, Helena attorney and territorial congressman. Reed reportedly served as Cavanaugh's prize fighter and strong-armed enforcer. Many stories exist of their drunken sprees, ruthless business practices, and brutality. "Their reputations were of hardened men whose sociopathic behavior ran unchecked."

In 2019, the Julia Hancock Chapter plans to clean and preserve the bronze DAR marker and again place it at the site, with help from Spika Welding of Lewistown.

SOURCES

- Historic monument records, Office of the Historian General, Washington D.C.
- *Record of Tablets and Markers Placed by Montana DAR 1908-1947*, by Mrs. Fred E. May
- *State Centennial History, MSSDAR*, by Iris McKinney Gray, Vol. V 1894-1994
- *Historical Sites Preserved and Markers Erected by MSSDAR and Its Chapters 1899-1977*, by Mrs. R.V. Love and Mrs. E.E. Bruno
- *MSSDAR 1982-1984 Pictorial Supplement to Historic Events of 1894-1977*, by Mrs. R.V. Love, Mrs. Sidney Groff and Miss Lorene Burks
- *Selling Your Father's Bones: America's 140-Year War Against the Nez Perce Tribe*, by Brian Schofield, New York: Simon & Schuster 2009
- *Great Falls Tribune* newspaper, Great Falls Montana, "Pair Operated Stage Station, Trading Post on Old Carroll Trail," Mar. 29, 1931
- National Register of Historic Places registration form, found at https://npgallery.nps.gov/GetAsset/72d2e2cf-9ede-4526-b07f-d5fa9e1f6b9b

*Reed and Bowles Stockade and Trading Post before reconstruction, 2017 photo*

*Historic photo of Reed and Bowles Stockade Trading Post, Lewistown Public Library, Culver/Brenner Collection, approx. 1970*

*Reed's Fort Post Office building (above) and DAR marker (below), 2017*

# 25. REED'S FORT POST OFFICE

Lewistown
GPS coordinates: 47.0585 | -109.4242

| | |
|---|---|
| **Commemorates** | First post office in central Montana, established January 6, 1881 |
| **Site Location** | 301 Casino Creek Drive, Lewistown, a National Register of Historic Places site |
| **Installed** | September 17, 1931 |
| **Wording** | "Reed's Fort Post Office. The first post office in central Montana was established here on January 6-1881 and named Reed's Fort after its first postmaster, Alonzo S. Reed. This building and site are presented to the city by the Lewistown Woman's Club. |
| | Marker placed and dedicated by Julia Hancock Chapter Daughters of the American Revolution, Lewistown, Montana, September 17-1931" |

## History

It was on September 17, 1931, that Julia Hancock Chapter, NSDAR erected and dedicated a two-by-three foot bronze marker at the site of the first post office in central Montana, Reed's Fort. This marker was crafted and donated by the Anaconda Copper Mining Company and rests on a native porphyry boulder brought from a nearby mountain canyon. The DAR chapter and Lewistown Woman's Club had restored the old post office to ensure it would remain a historic site in its original location. Lewistown schools closed for the occasion, which was also Constitution Day, for the 3:30 ceremony. State Historical Society Librarian and Historian David Hilger accepted the marker on behalf of the Historical Society and Mrs. E.A. Long of the Lewistown Woman's Club presented the building and site to the city. Mayor Stewart McConochie accepted the building on behalf of the city of Lewistown.

The Reed's Fort Post Office, established on January 6, 1881, is one of the oldest buildings in Lewistown and today is the only remaining building from Alonzo Reed's Reedsfort Homestead. It operated in the log building until August 24, 1885, when the post office moved to the T.C. Power Company store. Reed and his partner John J. Bowles ran the first trading post nearby in the Judith Basin from 1875 to 1880 and Reed was likely responsible for enticing the Metis from the Milk River area to settle in the Judith Basin in 1879. Reed's homestead, store, and post office supplanted the trading post.

The post office building is significant because it was built by Mose LaTray, a Metis carpenter originally from the Milk River area along the Canada-U.S. border and one of nearly 300 Metis who settled on Big Spring Creek between 1879 and 1880. The Red River Metis who settled there were known for their building expertise, especially their Red River Carts, but also as one of the few native tribes of the northern plains in the 1870s and 1880s to build and maintain permanent homes. Reed's Fort Post Office is one of only a few documented Metis buildings that still stand in North America and still reflect the traditions of Metis builders and the frontier architecture of a Montana territorial post office.

Reed's Fort Post Office stands less than 100 feet south of Little Casino Creek, one of two creeks named by the settlers in 1873. In the fall of 1873, businessmen Nelson Story and Charles W. Hoffman retained Peter Koch to travel north from Bozeman with a bull train of materials to "build, stock and manage" a trading post. Koch chose to place the new camp on the west side of Big Spring Creek, just north of Little Casino Creek and named it Fort Sherman.

As Koch later related,

*A site was selected just below the mouth of Big Casino Creek, on the south bank of Big Spring Creek, and when the ox train with the goods and supplies had arrived I built there, during November and December, 1873, the first permanent houses within the Judith Basin. While waiting in idleness for the arrival of the train, the boys put in most of their time with an old deck of cards, playing casino, and we accordingly named the creek we were camped on 'Big Casino' and a little spring creek just below 'Little Casino,' and I was much amused years after on seeing Colonel Ludlow's map that these names had been perpetuated.*

After DAR's 1931 restoration work, Reed's Fort Post Office was restored again in 1970 by a local volunteer group. While changed somewhat in appearance since it was built, the old building reflects its period of operation from 1880 to 1885 and has retained its builder's integrity of design, materials, and workmanship. The majority of the building's materials are intact, and the replacement logs and woodwork are in keeping with the originals. The roof material, door, and window sashes have been replaced in kind to resemble the original and appear much as they did when the post office was first photographed in a deteriorated condition in the 1920s. The 1970 restoration used most of the original building logs with only the lower bottom logs replaced due to rot. The corner notching was also altered in some cases in order to repair rotted areas. While some of the replacement logs and corner notching do not display the skillful notching original to Mose LaTray's workmanship, the work of his grandson Les LaTray was executed carefully and the overall design and materials of the original building were fully retained.

**SOURCES**

- Historic monument records, Office of the Historian General, Washington D.C.
- *Record of Tablets and Markers Placed by Montana DAR 1908-1947*, by Mrs. Fred E. May
- *Historical Sites Preserved and Markers Erected by MSSDAR and Its Chapters 1899-1977*, by Mrs. R.V. Love and Mrs. E.E. Bruno
- *State Centennial History, MSSDAR*, by Iris McKinney Gray, Vol. V 1894-1994
- *MSSDAR 1982-1984 Pictorial Supplement to Historic Events of 1894-1977*, by Mrs. R.V. Love, Mrs. Sidney Groff and Miss Lorene Burks
- *Great Falls Tribune* newspaper, Great Falls Montana, "Site of First Lewistown Postoffice Will Be Marked at Event on Thursday," Sept. 13, 1931, pg. 4
- *The Missoulian* newspaper, Missoula Montana, "Tablet Marking Site of First Lewistown Postoffice Unveiled," Sept. 18, 1931, pg. 7
- *The Montana Standard* newspaper, Butte Montana, "Early Postoffice Site at Lewistown Marked," Sept. 18, 1931, pg. 16
- Unidentified newspaper, "D.A.R. of Lewistown to Dedicate Postoffice Marker, Ceremony to be Carried Out on Constitution Day, September 17, at the Site of Old Reedsfort Post Office – Schools to Close for This Occasion – Hilger Invited," pg. 8
- National Register of Historic Places registration form, cited at http://www.waymarking.com/waymarks/WMWRD0_Reeds_Fort_Post_Office_Lewistown_MT

*Article in Great Falls Tribune, Sepember 13, 1931*

*Teigen School display inside museum, 2017*

# 26. Teigen School

Lewistown
GPS coordinates: 47.0709 | -109.4141

| | |
|---|---|
| **Commemorates** | Era of one-room schools |
| **Site Location** | *Original*: Symmes Park, Lewistown |
| | *Current*: Building no longer exists; instead, there is a Teigen School exhibit at Lewistown's Central Montana Museum |
| **Installed** | *Site dedicated*: July 3, 1976 |
| | *DAR marker installed*: September 17, 1983 |
| **Wording** | "Teigen School District 134 1914 - 1935 Donated by Teigen Family to Julia Hancock Chapter Daughters of the American Revolution Dedicated 1976" |

## History

In 1973, Julia Hancock Chapter, NSDAR began a project of finding a one-room rural school that they could move into Lewistown and preserve for future generations. After many miles of travel across many months, the chapter found old Teigen School and deemed its size to be satisfactory. The chapter contacted Norwegian immigrant rancher

Mons Teigen, who built the school in 1914 and still owned the building about donating it. He and his family agreed and deeded it to the Julia Hancock Chapter. The chapter took on the project of getting the school moved and repaired as a Bicentennial project. The chapter opened the school each spring to local teachers to conduct model classes in the same manner as taught at the turn of the century.

The school was moved to Central Montana Museum grounds in Lewistown and dedicated on July 3, 1976. On that occasion, the first teacher of the school, Miss Louise Smith (later Mrs. Bill Beedie) and two pupils from the school's first year, Amelia and John Luebke, were present. Marion Vinge, a pupil who attended the school in its final year of 1936, also participated in the 1976 ceremony.

From the beginning of the project, the chapter wanted to have a bell on the building, so again they began a search. Tony Tuss offered a bell if the chapter could install a tower in which to hang it. But, due to lack of funds, this project was delayed for several years. Then, in spring of 1983, Mr. Tuss agreed to build the tower, enlisting help from others. He installed the bell in the tower and placed it upon the school roof.

For the September 17, 1983, dedication ceremony, Julia Hancock Chapter Regent Mrs. Ramon Eatinger was mistress of ceremonies. The program included brief talks by NSDAR Honorary Vice President General Miss Marjorie Stevenson, Montana State Regent Mrs. Jess T. Schwidde, and Honorary State Regent Miss E. Lorene Burks. Special recognition was given to Mr. Tuss by Mrs. McVey and the official dedication of the marker was made by Mrs. Eatinger.

At the time, the Teigen School was the only DAR-owned building in Montana. It is included in *Historic and Memorial Buildings of the*

*Daughters of the American Revolution* compiled by Mollie Summerville in 1979, published by the NSDAR, Washington, D.C.

The Teigen School building no longer exists. In 2006 when the Central Montana Museum was building an addition, it found that the school's foundation had deteriorated to the point that the building could not be restored, so had to be torn down. The school's contents have been preserved inside the museum and a schoolhouse display has been included at the museum.

SOURCES
- History by Mrs. Lucile McVey, Past Regent of Julia Hancock Chapter
- Historic monument records, Office of the Historian General, Washington D.C.
- *State Centennial History, MSSDAR*, by Iris McKinney Gray, Vol. V 1894-1994
- *MSSDAR 1982-1984 Pictorial Supplement to Historic Events of 1894-1977*, by Mrs. R.V. Love, Mrs. Sidney Groff and Miss Lorene Burks

*Teigen School display inside museum, 2017*

*First Lewis and Clark trail marker, 2017*

# 27. First Lewis and Clark Trail Marker

Livingston
GPS coordinates: 45.66116547 | -110.56421152

| | |
|---|---|
| **Commemorates** | The trail where Captain Clark camped on his return journey from the Pacific Northwest |
| **Site Location** | *Original:* Facing the railroad tracks of the Northern Pacific Railway Livingston depot |
| | *Current*: Turned to face the road (in the park west of the depot, now a museum) |
| **Installed** | October 23, 1908 |
| **Wording** | "Trail of Lewis & Clark. This point was passed July 17, 1806. Marked Yellowstone Park Chapter D.A.R. October 23, 1908" |

## History

On October 23, 1908, the Yellowstone Park Chapter, NSDAR dedicated this boulder on the spot where Captain Clark camped on his return journey from the Pacific Northwest. The inscription on it commemorates the Lewis and Clark Expedition and is the first of Montana DAR's markers to be placed in honor of the Expedition.

In July, the Yellowstone Park Chapter made a "considerable sum" from an exhibit of "antique articles … of educational and artistic value." With this money and money from an assessment on the members of the chapter, the marker was purchased. According to October 10, 1908, chapter meeting minutes, there was:

> …progress made in finding a 'marker' for the Lewis and Clark Trail, Mrs. Scheuber having found a boulder, and the stone cutter having come down in his price from $130 to $18, the possibilities of placing the stone by the 23$^{rd}$ seem more encouraging.

The boulder, marking the spot where Captain Clark camped on his return journey from the Pacific Northwest, was placed close to the Northern Pacific Railway spur to Gardiner, near the Billman Creek crossing just south of Livingston in the Yellowstone River Canyon. Its placement was so it could be read from trains entering or leaving the station. The site was selected upon the authority of Olin D. Wheeler, historian for the Northern Pacific Railway. Mr. Wheeler made a trip through the West, following portions of the Lewis and Clark Trail and located the spot where Captain Clark camped on his return from the Northwest.

In 1912, the Yellowstone Park Chapter voted to move the boulder to a more visible location in the Northern Pacific Depot Park in downtown Livingston, where it remains today. Over the years, the boulder tipped to one side and during the 1994-96 term of Chapter Regent Mrs. Robert L. (Sharon) McIlhattan of Mt. Hyalite Chapter, the boulder was lifted, placed on a concrete base, and rededicated.

The 1908 dedication of this monument was just five months after the first marker erected by any Montana DAR chapter, the Spanish-American War Memorial, by the Silver Bow Chapter in Butte.

SOURCES

- Historic monument records, Office of the Historian General, Wash. D.C.
- *Record of Tablets and Markers Placed by Montana DAR 1908-1947*, by Mrs. Fred E. May
- *State Centennial History, MSSDAR*, by Iris McKinney Gray, 1894-1994
- *Historical Sites Preserved and Markers Erected by MSSDAR and Its Chapters, 1899-1977*, by Mrs. R.V. Love and Mrs. E.E. Bruno
- *MSSDAR 1982-1984 Pictorial Supplement to Historic Events of 1894-1977*, by Mrs. R.V. Love, Mrs. Sidney Groff and Miss Lorene Burks
- *The Butte Daily Post* newspaper, Butte Montana, "Monument to Mark Explorers' Camp on Yellowstone," Oct. 16, 1908, pg. 1
- *The Butte Daily Post* newspaper, Butte Montana, "Historic Site Marked by Livingston D.A.R.," Oct. 23, 1908, pg. 1
- *The Butte Miner* newspaper, Butte Montana, "First Marking of Historic Trail of Lewis and Clark," Oct. 24, 1908, pg. 1
- *Yellowstone Monitor* newspaper, Glendive Montana, "Marking the Trail of First Pioneers," Oct. 29, 1908, pg. 1
- *The American Monthly Magazine* (DAR), Sept. 1909, pps. 798-801

*First Lewis and Clark Trail marker at current site, 2017*

*Travelers' Rest marker (above) and site (below), 2017*

## 28. Travelers' Rest

Lolo
GPS coordinates: 46.753224 | -114.089975

| | |
|---|---|
| **Commemorates** | Lewis and Clark campsite both on the outward and return trips |
| **Site Location** | 1 mile south of Lolo off of US Route 93; a Montana State Park and National Historic Landmark |
| **Installed** | October 9, 1925 |
| **Wording** | "Travellers Rest. Bitter Root Chapter Daughters of the American Revolution Missoula Montana dedicate this marker to Captains Lewis and Clark, Sacajawea, their inspiration and guide and the brave men of the Trans-Mississippi Expedition who encamped on Lo Lo Creek September 10 - 1805. Ordway, Gass, Pryor, Windsor, Gibson, Shields, Willard, McNeal, Wiser, Lepage, Howard, Potts, Labiche, Colter, Hall, Collins, Werner, Frazier, Shannon, Cruzatte, Bratton, Thompson, Whitehouse, Fields Brothers, Drouillard, Goodrich, Chaboneau husband of Sacajawea, Baptiste their baby and York the slave. Dedicated October 9 1925" |

# History

On October 9, 1925, the Montana DAR closed their state conference in Missoula with the dedication at Travelers' Rest of a bronze marker set on a six-foot granite boulder. A crowd of 200 witnessed the ceremonies which began with a salute to the flag. Miss Anne M. Lang, Vice President General DAR, the first of the afternoon's speakers, said:

> *The marker, so fittingly placed to honor the intrepid men of the 1805-6 expedition into the Oregon territory, carries the whispers of that brave land. They say 'We have passed by here. Forget us not.' And let us not forget them, but through them remember our duty to our republic, the republic which their achievements made possible.*

State Regent Mrs. Verne D. Caldwell's speech was of the growing consciousness of America's early history, of the growing movement to preserve and mark spots of historic importance, and of the importance of such markers. Another speaker, President Charles H. Clapp of the University of Montana, said that he hoped that the monument would inspire the youth of Montana in "their spirit of devotion and social obligation to their country and in striving for the individual development for which the country stands."

The marker was presented to Missoula County, represented by R.R. Wilbur, chair of the Board of County Commissioners, by Mrs. J.M. Keith, Bitter Root Chapter, NSDAR regent. The unveiling was by Miss Barbara Nelson and Mr. John M. Griswold, children of DAR members.

The DAR marker, a bronze tablet donated by the Anaconda Copper Mining Company set into a six-ton granite boulder. The

Travelers' Rest marker is the only permanent marker that carries the names of the entire personnel list of the Lewis and Clark Expedition.

On September 9, 1805, before beginning the arduous passage across the Bitterroot Mountains, the Expedition camped at a spot Lewis and Clark named "Travellers Rest." It was a site long used by Native peoples, notably the Salish. The next day, Clark wrote:

> *Concluded to Delay to day and make Some observations, as at this place the rout which we are to prosue will pass up the Travelers rest Creek, The day proved fair and we took equal altitudes & Some luner observations. The Latd. 46° 48' 28" as the guide report that no game is to be found on our rout for a long ways, ads an addition to the cause of our delay to precure Some meat, despatched all our hunters in different directions, to hunt the Deer which is the only large game to be found.*

On the morning of September 11, the Expedition broke camp and continued westward into the mountains on the Lolo Trail. They returned to the area on June 30, 1806, and camped for three nights. Upon the July 3 departure, Clark took a contingent to explore the Yellowstone River, while Lewis headed for the Missouri and Marias rivers.

The boulder has an interesting history. Mrs. A. J. Gibson of the Bitter Root Chapter, NSDAR and her Committee for the Preservation of Historic Spots had been charged with finding a suitable stone on which to place it. Aided by her husband, a great supporter of the project, she located an excellent boulder at Elk Park (northeast of Butte, 150 miles away). The cost of getting the boulder to a loading platform was $30 and the freight to Missoula another $40. The boulder was then transported to Lolo and while unloading it, the workmen dropped the boulder. At that point, the boulder's cost totaled $120. While the chapter was shocked, they "whole-heartedly endorsed the finding of a second stone, as much that the arduous efforts of the Gibsons, so freely given, might now end in futility, as for the desire to make use of this most handsome and historic marker." The second stone ended up costing $150. In all, the Bitter Root Chapter ended up with a deficit of $120. Mrs. Gibson and Mrs. J.M. Keith each personally loaned the chapter $60 to cover the debt and it was some years later that the chapter was able to repay "our civic-minded members for their aid."

Added to the cost, there was tension between the community of Lolo and the placement of the marker, which was seen as intervention by outside communities, "and all efforts by the Committee to placate them were unavailing." The County Commissioners gave permission for a store to be built on the right of way to the road (at the spot already occupied by the marker) and sanctioned moving the stone adjacent to the store, where it became a "repository of all the refuse and litter usually to be found outside the doors of a small country store." Later, Highway 93 was put through, and the stone again had to be moved—but closer to the original campsite.

In November 1977, the Field Maintenance Division of the State Highway Department located the marker. It is still in the original setting but is not visible from the highway, as the highway has been moved.

In the summer of 2002, archaeologists found evidence of the Corps of Discovery's visit to the area, including a trench latrine tainted with mercury, fire hearths, and lead used to repair and manufacture firearms. The discovery makes Travelers' Rest the only campsite on the Lewis and Clark Trail with physical evidence of the Expedition. It is on the

National Register of Historic Places and Montana has created a state park, Travelers' Rest State Park, to commemorate the location.

Recognizing the importance of this historic marker, in 2019 the Bitter Root Chapter allocated $800 toward its refurbishment by Loken Historic Preservation LLC of Missoula. The chapter celebrated the newly-preserved marker on May 11, 2019.

*(**Note 1**: The spelling of this site has changed over the years. Initially called "Travellers Rest," the name is now spelled "Travelers' Rest.")*

*(**Note 2**: Sacajawea's husband's name is shown in historic records spelled two ways– Chaboneau and later, Charbonneau. The 1928 marker uses the older spelling.)*

### Sources

- Historic monument records, Office of the Historian General, Washington D.C.
- *Record of Tablets and Markers Placed by Montana DAR 1908-1947*, by Mrs. Fred E. May
- *State Centennial History, MSSDAR*, by Iris McKinney Gray, Vol. V 1894-1994
- *Historical Sites Preserved and Markers Erected by MSSDAR and Its Chapters 1899-1977*, by Mrs. R.V. Love and Mrs. E.E. Bruno
- *MSSDAR 1982-1984 Pictorial Supplement to Historic Events of 1894-1977*, by Mrs. R.V. Love, Mrs. Sidney Groff and Miss Lorene Burks
- *The Butte Miner* newspaper, "Splendid Historical Tablet To Be Unveiled Friday, October 9," Oct. 4, 1925, p. 52
- *The Missoulian* newspaper, "Tablet Dedicated by Montana DAR," Oct. 10, 1925, pg. 1
- *The Choteau Acantha* newspaper, Choteau, Montana, "Montana D.A.R. Dedicates Marker In Honor of Lewis and Clark on the Lolo Trail West of Missoula," Oct. 29, 1925
- Travelers' Rest, New State Park Jewel in Missoula County, at https://montanahistoriclandscape.com/tag/lewis-and-clark-national-historic-trail/
- National Park Service, http://traveler-s-rest-mt.htm
- History of the Bitter Root Chapter, by Tina Parker, May 11, 1957

*Boot Hill Cemetery marker (above) and site (below), 2017*

# 29. Boot Hill Cemetery

Powderville, southeast of Miles City
GPS coordinates: 45.759375 | -105.124321

| | |
|---|---|
| **Commemorates** | Cemetery at Deadwood Crossing, the old stage crossing of Powder River from Fort Keogh to Fort Meade |
| **Site Location** | One mile north of Powderville, 60 miles southeast of Miles City |
| **Installed** | July 4, 1976 |
| **Wording** | "Boot Hill Cemetery 1870 Deadwood Crossing Erected by Powder River Chapter DAR July 4, 1976" |

## History

The July 4, 1976, marker dedication was a bicentennial salute by the Powder River Chapter, NSDAR. The chapter said, "We, Powder River Chapter, National Society of the Daughters of the American Revolution, join with this community in establishing a marker on this historic site." DAR and the Powderville community held a ceremony at 4:30 p.m. to dedicate a bronze plaque on native sandstone on the historic route.

When stage coaches travelled the trails from Fort Keogh, Montana, to Fort Meade, South Dakota, this crossing at the Powder River was known as Deadwood Crossing. It was later called Elkhorn and finally became Powderville. There is a river ford nearby and, at one time, a ferry served stage coaches and other transportation of frontier travelers. When Dick Richardson carried mail on this route, he crossed the Powder River in a bull boat, which was a buffalo hide stretched across a framework to form a tub shaped boat. The trail served as a mail and freight route, frequented heavily by horse thieves and highwaymen, but lightly by other travelers.

The stage trail started at Fort Keogh, was mapped as a telegraph line in 1878, and ended at the Fort Meade cavalry post, established to protect early miners and settlers.

The cemetery was founded in 1872. Its name, "Boot Hill" is a common name for old-time cemeteries; the U.S. has at least 40 cemeteries of that name.

SOURCES

- Historic monument records, Office of the Historian General, Washington D.C.
- *State Centennial History, MSSDAR*, by Iris McKinney Gray, Vol. V 1894-1994
- *Historical Sites Preserved and Markers Erected by MSSDAR and Its Chapters 1899-1977*, by Mrs. R.V. Love and Mrs. E.E. Bruno
- *MSSDAR 1982-1984 Pictorial Supplement to Historic Events of 1894-1977*, by Mrs. R.V. Love, Mrs. Sidney Groff and Miss Lorene Burks
- *The Billings Gazette* newspaper, Billings Montana, "Freedom Picnic in Broadus Sunday," July 2, 1976, pg. 9

*Dedication of DAR historical marker at Travelers' Rest, October 9, 1925
With permission, Montana Historical Society Research Center Photography
Archives 957-641*

*Fort Keogh Officer Quarters marker (above and on boulder below) and restored building (below), 2017*

# 30. Fort Keogh Officer Quarters

Miles City
GPS coordinates: 46.402766 | -105.86299

| | |
|---|---|
| **Commemorates** | The only remaining building of the original Fort Keogh |
| **Site Location** | In front of the Fort Keogh officer quarters building at the Range Riders Museum |
| **Installed** | June 19, 1976 |
| **Wording** | "Officers' Quarters 1876 Fort Keogh Placed by Powder River Chapter DAR June 19, 1976" |

## History

On June 19, 1976, the Powder River Chapter, NSDAR placed a bronze marker mounted on a native Powder River boulder at the Range Riders Museum in Miles City. It was installed for the bicentennial of the Declaration of Independence (and was dedicated at the 100th anniversary of the founding of Fort Keogh).

Shortly after the Battle of the Little Big Horn on June 25, 1876, General Nelson A. Miles was sent to the area with orders to establish a fort. He picked a strategic site at the confluence of the Yellowstone and Tongue Rivers from which to conduct a military campaign against the Indians. On July 22, 1876, Congress established the Fort Keogh Military Reservation, known then as the Cantonment on Tongue River. The fort was later moved a mile west and renamed Fort Myles Keogh; it was established as a permanent Army post in 1877. (Captain Keogh died with General George Custer at the Battle of Little Big Horn; it was his wounded horse "Comanche" that was the sole survivor of the battle.)

The fort contained five infantry companies and six cavalry companies who protected the frontier settlement of Miles City and enabled area cattlemen to flourish without fear of rustlers or marauding Indians. It was from this fort that General Nelson A. Miles and his men went to the Bear Paw Mountains and affected Chief Joseph's surrender. General Miles' mission was a success—by the early 1880's, most tribes had surrendered and moved onto reservations.

In 1907, all infantry troops were removed and two years later, Fort Keogh became a Remount Station and supplied thousands of horses for World War I. In 1922, the Army relinquished claim to the fort and began its withdrawal. Finally, by an Act of Congress on April 15, 1924, the station was turned over to the U.S. Department of Agriculture which now uses the Fort Keogh site as a beef cattle research facility.

In the late 1800s, the fort contained about 120 buildings, but today only four survive. Just one of the officer quarters buildings survived and it was moved from its original location to the Tongue River Bridge leading into Miles City's main street with financial support of the

Powder River Chapter whose members wished to save at least part of the old fort from extinction. The building now houses part of the Range Rider Museum's collection. It is a duplex in which the left side is largely restored, while the right side awaits a restoration by the museum.

SOURCES

- Historic monument records, Office of the Historian General, Wash. D.C.
- *State Centennial History, MSSDAR*, by Iris McKinney Gray, 1894-1994
- *Historical Sites Preserved and Markers Erected by MSSDAR and Its Chapters 1899-1977*, by Mrs. R.V. Love and Mrs. E.E. Bruno
- *MSSDAR 1982-1984 Pictorial Supplement to Historic Events of 1894-1977*, by Mrs. R.V. Love, Mrs. Sidney Groff and Miss Lorene Burks
- "Fort Keogh," United States Department of Agriculture, at https://www.ars.usda.gov/plains-area/miles-city-mt/larrl/docs/fort-keogh-history/

*Historic photo of prior view taken about 1963. Shows porches, view to the SW Library of Congress, Call # HABS MONT,9-MILCI,3-B-1*

*Montana Real Daughter Caroline Reed Stone, DAR grave marker, 2017*

# 31. MONTANA REAL DAUGHTER CAROLINE REED STONE

Shelby
GPS coordinates: n/a

| | |
|---|---|
| **Commemorates** | Caroline Reed Stone's status as a DAR Real Daughter |
| **Site Location** | Mountain View Cemetery, Shelby |
| **Installed** | June 12, 2010 |
| **Wording** | "Caroline Reed Stone 1826-1923 NSDAR Real Daughter. Marker placed by the Montana State Society, NSDAR May 2010" |

## About "DAR Real Daughters"

All Daughters of the American Revolution are descended from Revolutionary War patriots and soldiers. A surprising number of daughters of America's first patriots were still alive in 1890 when DAR was founded. In fact, 770 women once held the distinction of being called "Real Daughters," DAR members just a single generation removed from the Revolutionary War. Many of these women were the youngest daughters of a large family or the result of a marriage late in life.

Not to be confused with the "daughter of a Revolutionary war soldier or patriot," a Real Daughter is distinguished by DAR because she was a DAR <u>member</u> as well as the actual daughter of a soldier or patriot. In the early years of the National Society, a DAR chapter who could name one or more of the 770 Real Daughters among its members was extremely proud of this living link to the American Revolution. Montana has two such Daughters– in addition to Caroline Reed Stone, another Real Daughter is buried in Montana, Orpha Zilpha Parke Bovee (in Glendive). *(See chapter titled "Montana Real Daughter Orpha Zilpha Parke Bovee.")*

## CAROLINE REED STONE, A REAL DAUGHTER

Caroline was born on February 17, 1826, in Portville, Cattaraugus County, New York, and died on January 21, 1923, at age 96, 11 months and 4 days. Her Revolutionary War Patriot father, Ebenezer Reed, was born in 1760 in Connecticut. He left his Tory home at age 16 and enlisted as a private, serving for two years with the Connecticut troops under Captains Bell, Brown, Warren and Stoddard and under Colonel Silliman. On October 3, 1832, he was granted a pension for over two years' actual service in the Connecticut troops. Caroline's mother, Polly Dickinson Reed, was Ebenezer's second wife (his first was Hannah Jones).

In 1855, Caroline married Eli Stone in Olean, Pratt County, New York. They moved to Minnesota to farm and lived there until 1904, when they moved to South Park, Washington to live with daughter Alma. In the 1920 U.S. Census, Caroline was recorded as living in

Spokane with a grandchild. She then moved to Shelby under the care of grandson E.J. Engle and lived in Shelby until her death. On January 22, 1923, she was buried in the Mountain View Cemetery in Shelby (Toole County).

Caroline was not a member of the Montana Society DAR but was a member of the Olean Chapter of New York. Her DAR application was officially approved on November 22, 1898 (#26202).

It was 86 years later, in mid-2009, that the National Society DAR approved a Real Daughter marker for Mrs. Stone at the urging of then-State Regent JoAnn Piazzola who wanted to ensure all Real Daughter graves in Montana were appropriately marked.

Caroline Reed Stone's marker dedication ceremony was held on June 12, 2010, at 1:00. It drew a crowd of 100 from Montana, Oregon, Washington and Colorado, including DAR officers, State Representative Roy Hollandsworth, Sons of the American Revolution members, and Children of the American Revolution members. Eight of Caroline Reed Stone's direct descendants attended, as well.

Black Eagle-Assinniboine Chapter, NSDAR Regent Benna Nichols McGeorge and the Montana State Society DAR planned the event. Following Boy Scout Troop 555's flag ceremony, State Regent JoAnn Piazzola and State Chaplain Barbara Delsigne led the marker dedication. In her comments, Mrs. Piazzola remarked:

> *...in this lone, secluded grave, apart and far across the miles from any kin, or kindred–sleeping the last long sleep–lies a Real Daughter of the American Revolution, the daughter of a compatriot of the immortal Washington.*

The marker was unveiled by Mrs. Stone's descendants, including DAR members Judy Wheeler, Robin Oos, Vergie Olson, and Marta Farrell. Afterwards, at an Elks Lodge reception, U.S. Senators Max Baucus' and Jon Tester's messages were read, and great-great-great-granddaughter Mrs. Oos and Marias Museum director Dean Hellinger presented family and area histories.

Caroline Reed Stone's DAR plaque is at her gravesite at the Mountain View Cemetery. Originally, she was buried in an unmarked grave, described as "north half of Lot 11, Section 10."

### Sources

- *DAR American Monthly Magazine*, April 1907, pps. 311-313
- *Daughters of the American Revolution Newsletter*, Sept./Oct. 2010, pg. 392
- State of Montana Bureau of Vital Statistics Certificate of Death, File #17, Jan. 22, 1923
- *The Shelby Promoter* newspaper, Shelby Montana, obituary, Jan. 1923
- *The Shelby Promoter* newspaper, Shelby Montana, photo, June 2010

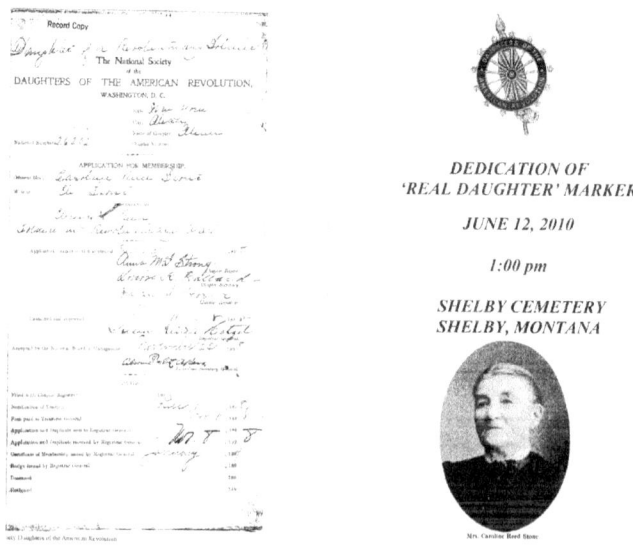

*Marker dedication program, 2010*

*Laura Tolman Scott article in The Dillon Examiner newspaper, April 3, 1929*

*Sacajawea monument with DAR marker on left side, current view, 2017*

# 32. SACAJAWEA MEMORIAL- THREE FORKS

Three Forks
GPS coordinates: 45.89521261 | -111.552661

| | |
|---|---|
| **Commemorates** | Sacajawea, the Indian woman who guided the Lewis and Clark Expedition |
| **Site Location** | On a small plot of ground in Three Forks near the Chicago, Milwaukee, St. Paul and Pacific Railroad; a statue was later added as well as a raised planting bed on which the statue sits |
| **Installed** | *Original*: October 2, 1914 |
| | *First rededication*: July 26, 1980 |
| | *Second rededication*: October 25, 2014 |
| **Wording** | "Sacajawea an Indian woman whose heroic courage steadfast devotion and splendid loyalty in acting as guide across the Rocky Mountains made it possible for the Lewis and Clark Expedition 1804-1806 to occupy so important a place in the history of this republic. Erected by the Montana Daughters of the American Revolution 1914" |

# History

On October 2, 1914, Montana State DAR placed a bronze tablet memorial to Sacajawea on a five-ton boulder near the Chicago, Milwaukee, St. Paul and Pacific Railroad station on a small plot of ground at Three Forks across from the Sacajawea Hotel. The marker, presented to Three Forks in the name of the Montana Society DAR, created Three Forks' first park. The tablet honored Sacajawea, the Lemhi Shoshone Indian woman who guided the Lewis and Clark Expedition through an uncharted wilderness in 1804-1806. Reportedly, one thousand people attended the marker's dedication and unveiling.

When DAR determined to erect a symbol of honor to Sacajawea, "a ferociously determined lady often credited for the very survival of Lewis and Clark and the success of that Expedition," the organization first approached the town of Livingston, but received little enthusiasm there. Mrs. Clinton H. Moore of Butte, chair of the marker committee working with Mrs. E. Broox Martin of Bozeman and Mrs. J.W. (Laura Tolman) Scott of Armstead, pushed for the monument. She went so far as dictating a letter to Montana U.S. Senator William A. Clark in which she stressed the historical importance of a marker and urged Sen. Clark to "heed her words." She also inquired as to how much it would take to finance the creation. As luck would have it, Sen. Clark gifted the bronze plaque and Three Forks' founder, J.Q. Adams, procured the massive boulder upon which to affix the plaque. The bronze marker was cast at the Henry Bonnard Bronze Co. in Mt. Vernon, New York (owned by Senator Clark).

On the day of the 1914 dedication, severe rain and thunder sent the crowds into Henslee's auditorium, where Rev. Thomas gave a "rousing invocation," followed by DAR State Regent Mrs. E.A. Morley who talked briefly about the monument's purpose. School children from across the area who traveled to be part of the ceremony joined in with several patriotic songs saluting Sacajawea.

On July 26, 1980, to celebrate the 175 years since the Expedition and its discovery of the Missouri River headwaters, DAR rededicated its 1914 marker and immediately afterwards, a flagpole at the Headwaters State Park in Trident. The 3:00 rededication ceremonies were led by DAR State Regent Mrs. Frank J. (Bonnie) Pickett. She later reported:

> *Thirty DAR members from six chapters–one from out of state– helped Mount Hyalite dedicate their flagpole at the Headwaters State Park and the Montana State Society DAR rededicate the Sacajawea state marker in the Three Forks Park. It was a beautiful Montana July day for the ceremonies as well as for the potluck picnic with the Montana Society Sons of the American Revolution, and the Lewis and Clark pageant in the outdoor setting at the Headwaters of the Missouri River State Park.*

Miss Kathy Gibson, a charter member of Valley of Flowers Children of the American Revolution, read the "Biography of Sacajawea." Other DAR chapters sent representatives (Anaconda, Beaverhead, Shining Mountain, Silver Bow), as did state and national DAR officers.

At 4:00 of that same day, July 26, attendees dedicated a flag pole at the Missouri Headquarters Park. The flag pole was given jointly by the Mount Hyalite Chapter, NSDAR and the Sons of the American

Revolution. Local Boy Scouts, the Three Forks Area Historical Society, and the Gallatin County Historical Society participated in both dedications.

In 2005, after years of fund-raising, the Three Forks Area Historical Society placed a statue of Sacajawea in Sacajawea Park next to the DAR marker. The statue is a 250-pound life-and-a-quarter-sized bronze that depicts Sacajawea in a sitting position holding her infant son, Pomp. Its "coming home" theme descends from when Sacajawea reached the Missouri River Headwaters at Three Forks in July 1805, and recognized the Tobacco Root Mountains to the southwest. (A Shoshone Indian, she had been kidnapped there and taken away by rival Hidatsa warriors to what is now North Dakota.)

On October 25, 2014, the Mount Hyalite Chapter sponsored a second marker rededication to celebrate the 100th centennial of the DAR marker's original placement. The celebration began at 10:30 a.m. at the Sacajawea Hotel, across the street from the marker and statue of Sacajawea, and ended with a catered luncheon. Guest speaker Charles Spray of the Gallatin Historical Society spoke on Sacajawea and local historian Patrick Finnegan spoke about the Patron Saints of Three Forks. The event was co-hosted by the Headwaters Heritage Museum and the Three Forks Area Historical Society.

SOURCES
- Historic monument records, Office of the Historian General, Wash. D.C.
- *Record of Tablets and Markers Placed by Montana DAR 1908-1947*, by Mrs. Fred E. May
- *State Centennial History, MSSDAR*, by Iris McKinney Gray, Vol. V 1894-1994
- *Historical Sites Preserved and Markers Erected by MSSDAR and Its Chapters 1899-1977*, by Mrs. R.V. Love and Mrs. E.E. Bruno
- *MSSDAR 1982-1984 Pictorial Supplement to Historic Events of 1894-1977*, by Mrs. R.V. Love, Mrs. Sidney Groff and Miss Lorene Burks

- *The Dillon Examiner* newspaper, Dillon Montana, "Tablet to Mark Historic Trail: Daughters of the American Revolution Are in Charge of the Work," Aug. 5, 1914
- *Saco Independent* newspaper, Saco Montana, "Montana Women Propose to Keep Memory of Sacajawea Green," Aug. 21, 1914
- *Belgrade News* newspaper, Belgrade Montana, "Long-awaited Sacajawea Statue Arrives in Three Forks," Apr. 1, 2005
- *Three Forks Herald* newspaper, Three Forks Montana, "Sacajawea Centennial Celebration is Saturday," Oct. 23, 2014

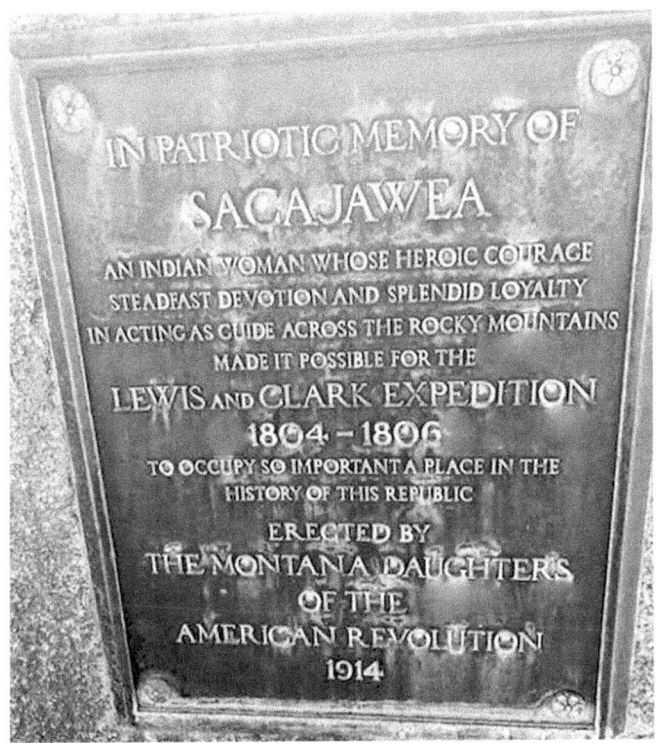

*Sacajawea DAR marker, 2017*

*Fort Logan Blockhouse DAR marker (above) and the blockhouse (below), 2017*

# 33. Fort Logan Blockhouse

Northwest of White Sulphur Springs
GPS coordinates: 46.678513 | -111.173753

| | |
|---|---|
| **Commemorates** | Historic Fort Logan |
| **Site Location** | 17 miles northwest of White Sulphur Springs on MT Highway 360, a National Register of Historic Places site |
| **Installed** | August 17, 1924 |
| **Wording** | "Original Block House. Part of Camp Baker established 1869. Post moved to present site 1870. Name changed to Fort Logan 1878 in honor of Captain William Logan killed by the Nez Perces Indians in the Battle of the Big Hole August 9 1877. Garrisoned as a military post 1869-1879. Abandoned by Government 1880. Restored and dedicated to posterity by Oro Fino Chapter Daughters of the American Revolution, Helena Montana August 17 1924" |

## History

On Sunday, August 17, 1924, Oro Fino Chapter, NSDAR placed and dedicated a bronze marker at the old Fort Logan Blockhouse which the chapter had restored. The tablet is believed to have been provided by the Anaconda Copper Mining Company, but is not labeled as such. The blockhouse and the land on which it stood had been given to the Oro Fino Chapter by subsequent land owner Charles Gaddis. (Years later it reverted back to donor Mr. Gaddis because of the distance from Helena to maintain it.)

At the 1924 dedication, the local newspaper noted:

*An immense crowd was present to witness the impressive ceremonies. It seemed that the citizenry of Meagher County was there en masse. Automobile parties were present from distant parts of the state, and a large delegation of pioneers and D.A.R. members and others from Helena were on the ground to pay their respect and honor to the memory of Captain Logan, and to help in the ceremonies that would preserve to posterity in Montana, this memorable landmark.*

In total, attendance was estimated at 1,500. By noon, over 1,000 attendees picnicked on the old parade grounds then attended the program which started at 1:15 p.m. It included Kalispell attorney Sidney M. Logan, son of Captain Logan, Governor Joseph N. Dixon, former Governor S.V. Stewart of Helena, and Congressman Scott Leavitt of Great Falls in addition to DAR State Regent Mrs. Verne D. Caldwell of Billings. DAR member Mrs. F. H. Johnson led the plaque dedication ceremony.

Fort Baker, as it was originally called, was established in November 1869 at the recommendation of Major General Winfield Scott Hancock, in command of the Department of the Dakota at that time. (General Hancock, a hero on the Union Side at the Battle of Gettysburg, later ran as the Democratic nominee for President against James A. Garfield, who defeated him in 1880.) The Fort was originally a sub-post of Fort Benton and was sited on the west bank of the Smith River from 1869-1870.

The second site was 10 miles south and was active 1870 to 1880. The primary reason for establishing the post was to protect miners (at Diamond City, Castle, and Copperopolis), local ranchers, and the Fort Benton freight route. The Fort's first commander was Captain George S. Hollister of the 7th Infantry.

Fort Baker's name was changed in 1878 to Fort Logan in honor of Captain William Logan, who was killed on August 9, 1877, by the Nez Perce Indians under Chief Joseph as the Battle of the Big Hole. This Indian fighter and hero of many wars was shot in the battle by a revengeful Indian woman. When his body was recovered, it was found stripped of uniform, scalped, and one little finger removed. On this finger, Captain Logan wore two rings–one mounted with various Masonic emblems, the other, a seal ring that had been in the family for generations. The seal was the family crest of the House of Bruce of Scotland, engraved and enameled on a violet-colored stone. It was a gift from his father when he started on his journey to America. Years later, the rings were recovered from the Indians, who did not attach significance to their value.

The Fort Logan Blockhouse is believed to be the only original of its kind still standing in the Northwest. The fort's buildings included quarters for 100 men, officers' quarters (two log buildings, one frame), a log hospital, two storehouses (one of which was adobe and was still standing in 1979 when extremely high winds blew in its walls), the blockhouse, and a two-story log building. The log blockhouse is unusually designed, with a square second floor set at 45-degree angle to the square plan of the first floor, so that it presents an eight-sided defensive structure. The wood was cut at the Moore Brothers' sawmill, a few miles north of the fort on the Smith River.

In late October 1880, when it was headquarters of two U.S. Infantry companies, the Fort was abandoned by order of The War Department and the garrison transferred to Fort Maginnis, near the Judith Mountains.

Judge William Gaddis, the post sutler, purchased the property soon after for $4,525 and started a ranch there, as well as continuing to operate the store and post office. In 1938, Mr. Charles Gaddis tried to interest the state of Montana in the blockhouse and original Fort Logan lands for a state park, but the state lacked the funds for its purchase and maintenance.

In 1946, Charles sold Fort Logan Ranch to Sidney and Arthur Berg who donated the blockhouse to the White Sulphur Springs Historical Society.

In 1962, the blockhouse was moved from its original location to the center of the fort's parade ground where it was set on a concrete base and again restored.

The Berg family maintains the Fort Logan Blockhouse and several other old military buildings on their property. The Bergs put a new roof on the old blockhouse in 2013.

On October 6, 1970, it was added to the National Register of Historic Places, site #70000360.

#### Sources
- Historic monument records, Office of the Historian General, Wash. D.C.
- *Record of Tablets and Markers Placed by Montana DAR 1908-1947*, by Mrs. Fred E. May
- *State Centennial History, MSSDAR*, by Iris McKinney Gray, 1894-1994

- *Historical Sites Preserved and Markers Erected by MSSDAR and Its Chapters 1899-1977*, by Mrs. R.V. Love and Mrs. E.E. Bruno
- *MSSDAR 1982-1984 Pictorial Supplement to Historic Events of 1894-1977*, by Mrs. R.V. Love, Mrs. Sidney Groff and Miss Lorene Burks
- *The Choteau Acantha* newspaper, Choteau Montana, "Historic Old Landmark is Dedicated to Posterity–Permanent Marker Placed on Block House at Site of Fort Logan," Aug. 28, 1924
- *The Dillon Examiner* newspaper, Dillon Montana, "Site of Ft. Logan is Dedicated by Oro Fino D.A.R.," Aug. 20, 1924
- *Mountains of Gold, Hills of Grass: A History of Meagher County*, by Lee Rostad, published by Bozeman Fork Publishing, 1994
- Library of Congress, "Fort Logan, Blockhouse, White Sulphur Springs, Meagher County, MT" (http://www.loc.gov/pictures/item/mt0029/)
- Fort Baker (Fort Logan) Block House, Written Historical and Descriptive Data, Office of Archeology and Historic Preservation, Washington D.C., prepared by John N. DeHaas, Jr., May 1967

*Fort Logan Blockhouse site, 2017*

*Camp Fortunate DAR marker, 1937*

*Beaverhead Rock historic photo–Beaverhead County Museum*
*(by C.W. "Bill" Bridenstine)*

# 34. LOST DAR MARKERS

As might be expected with the passing of time, some Montana DAR historic markers have been destroyed or simply lost. Of the original 70 DAR historical markers, 32 fall into that category.

Looking at the markers that have survived, it is evident that sheer size and marker type contribute to their permanence. Early markers were typically set in six- and eight-ton boulders or massive cement slabs, with two- by three-foot heavy bronze plaques firmly installed. It was the wooden signs and small metal markers that did not last more than five to ten years. For these, little historic information remains.

## Beaverhead Rock

| | |
|---|---|
| **GPS coordinates** | 45.38333 \| -112.40690 |
| **Commemorated** | Ancient landmark used by Indians, the Lewis and Clark Expedition, and pioneer settlers |
| **Site location** | 12 miles south of Twin Bridges on State Highway 41; a Montana State Park and on the National Register of Historic Places |
| **Installed** | August 10, 1955 |
| **Marker lost** | Due to theft and later, to deterioration of wooden replacement sign |

# History

On the evening of August 10, 1955, "against the background of a flaming Western sunset," the Beaverhead Chapter, NSDAR dedicated a marker to commemorate historic Beaverhead Rock, also known as "Point of Rocks" This was a cooperative venture. The bronze marker was donated by the Anaconda Copper Mining Company. A state highway department maintenance crew placed the bronze tablet onto a six-ton native mountain boulder. The Beaverhead County Commissioners transported the boulder to the Beaverhead Rock site on Highway 41 on the border between Beaverhead and Madison Counties.

Among dignitaries attending the ceremony were Director of the Montana Historical Society K. Ross Toole, Beaverhead Chapter Regent Mrs. Ike Rife who welcomed the crowd of 100, and State Senator J.S. Brenner who accepted the marker on behalf of the state of Montana. Miss Jean Bishop, chair of DAR chapter's Marker Committee, talked about the Expedition's experiences in the region.

Historical records are unclear in the exact wording of the inscription. One version says:

> *As the Lewis and Clark Expedition came up the river August 8, 1805, Sacajawea pointed out to Captain Meriwether Lewis the Great Rock, saying her people called it the "Beaver's Head." Captain Clark with the main party passed this spot August 10. This ancient Landmark gives its name to this section of the Jefferson River, longest fork of the Missouri and to the largest county in the State of Montana.*

The second version is slightly different:

*As the Lewis and Clark Expedition came up the river August 8, 1805, Sacajawea pointed out to Captain Meriwether Lewis the Great Rock, saying her people called it the 'Beaverhead.' Captain Clark with the main party passed this spot August 10. This ancient landmark gives its name to the stream flowing into the Jefferson River and also the County and Valley are named Beaverhead.*

The DAR marker was erected to commemorate Lewis and Clark's trip up the Beaverhead River in August 1805. It was at this point that Sacajawea told Captain Clark, "This is the land of my people." *The Mineral Independent* newspaper (Superior, Montana) reported,

*A celebration of more than unusual interest was held at Beaverhead Rock, famous landmark, 12 miles south of Twin Bridges and 16 miles north of Dillon a few days ago, under the auspices of the Beaverhead Chapter of the Daughters of the American Revolution, to commemorate the service of Sacajawea, the Indian woman who was the guide and savior of Lewis and Clark…*

The 1955 DAR marker dedication was not the first time that DAR had commemorated the site. On September 5, 1921, the Beaverhead Chapter held a 12:30 p.m. ceremony attended by a crowd of 300 along the banks of the Beaverhead River to mark the spot where Sacajawea recognized her homeland. State Regent Mrs. A.L. Anderson delivered an address titled, "The Aims of the Local, State and National D.A.R." Historian Dr. Frank H. Garver of Montana State Normal College gave a talk titled "The Beaverhead Rock in History," and DAR member Mrs. Laura Tolman Scott's presentation was "The Marker," then local resident and pioneer John Bishop told stories of early days in the county. The marker, one of six donated by the Beaverhead County commissioners, was plate steel with welded letters finished in silver and black. (The other sites marked with these markers were reported to be Rattlesnake Cliffs, Sarvice Berrie Vallie, Indian Head Mountain, Shoshone Cove and Camp Fortunate, all placed during the summer of 1921.) The Beaverhead Rock metal marker was planned to be set in masonry and concrete pyramid "which will be of artistic design and mark fittingly the most important spot on the famous trail of the pioneers of 1805." (This did not occur.)

During the 1960s, Beaverhead Rock's historic importance was preserved when Beaverhead Chapter's Mrs. Elfreda (J. Fred) Woodside persuaded U.S. Senator Mike Mansfield to sponsor it as a national landmark. (The site is on the National Register of Historic Places.) Montana's Governor Tim Babcock followed suit, setting it aside as a state landmark as well. These designations saved the site from further damage than had been done when the rock face had been blasted and the rock used for rip-rap on the river and a canal.

In the early 1970s, Beaverhead Rock's owners offered to sell the landmark to the state Fish and Game Department for $60,000, the value as set by an appraisal by Lewis and Clark historian E.E. MaGilvra of Butte. The Montana legislature voted $30,000 for its purchase in 1971, an amount matched by the National Park Service. When the papers were drawn up for a title transfer, the Montana Institute of Appraisers valued the rock only for its value as rip-rap and the remaining 84 acres as agricultural land, a total appraised value of just $20,000. The owners, Mr. and Mrs. Norman Ashcraft, refused to sell the property for that amount and refused again after they were offered $40,000 (less $1,850 for the appraisal and $193 for legal fees). The state started condemnation proceedings on the property, while the Ashcrofts began blasting stone for river stabilization. After more court battles, the Ashcrofts received $72,500 for the property. The long legal dispute ended in December 1975 when the 30-acre Beaverhead Rock State Park came into being.

In a 1972 interview with *Montana Standard* newspaper writer Helen Fenton, local resident August Mailey, who was born and raised near Beaverhead Rock, said that Lewis and Clark "left their mark" on the landmark. Mailey recalled an inscription painted on the rocks "on what we called the little point and parallels the present road." Mailey's father blasted the rock upon which the inscription sat while working for Mr. Washington Nyhard in order to make room for an irrigation ditch. Mr. Mailey said, "They did not pay so much attention to history when my father did that blasting, but he always felt bad about it."

In 1971, when Chapter Regent Mrs. Virginia Lee (August) Schreiber learned the 1955 bronze tablet marking Beaverhead Rock had been stolen, she began negotiations with the Montana Highway Department to replace it with a standard historical marker. She then surveyed all the DAR markers that had been placed in Beaverhead County for the Montana's Markers Commission, which typically placed one such historical marker each year.

In 1976, the Montana Highway Department replaced the DAR Beaverhead Rock marker with a wooden historical marker in March. Then, on May 4, 1976, at 10:00 a.m., the Beaverhead Chapter DAR dedicated the replacement sign, which bore the same legend as the original marker. The wooden sign bore these words:

> *Beaverhead Rock. August 10, 1805, members of the Lewis and Clark Expedition pushed their way up the Jefferson River's tributaries toward the Continental Divide and the Pacific Ocean beyond. Toward afternoon they sighted what Clark called a "remarkable Clift" to the west. Sacajawea (or, as Lewis spelled it*

*Sah-cah-gar we-ah), their Indian guide for this portion of the trip, said her tribe called the large promontory 'Beaver's Head.'*

*Both Lewis and Clark agreed on the rock's likeness to the fur bearing animal and recorded the name in their journals. They continued south only to encounter a heavy rain and hail storm. 'The men defended themselves from the hail by means of the willow bushes but all the party got perfectly wet,' Lewis said. They camped upstream from the Beaver's head, enjoyed freshly killed deer meat, then pushed on the next day.*

*Beaverhead Rock served as an important landmark not only for Lewis and Clark, but also for the trappers, miners, and traders who followed them into the vicinity. It is the namesake for the county in which it is now located, retaining the same appearance that inspired Sacajawea and her people to name it centuries ago.*

In addition to local media, the 1976 marker dedication ceremony drew local dignitaries and DAR members. Mrs. Roger Poff and Mrs. Elfreda Woodside of the Beaverhead Chapter DAR conducted the ceremonies; Montana DAR Vice Regent Mrs. Orrion Pilon dedicated the marker; and Jack Brown of the Montana Highway Department represented the state. Also attending were State Senator Frank Hazelbaker, Supervisor of the Dillon Bureau of Land Management Office Jack McIntosh, and other BLM personnel and DAR members.

SOURCES
- Historic monument records, Office of the Historian General, Wash. D.C.
- *Record of Tablets and Markers Placed by Montana DAR 1908-1947*, by Mrs. Fred E. May
- *State Centennial History, MSSDAR*, by Iris McKinney Gray, 1894-1994
- *Historical Sites Preserved and Markers Erected by MSSDAR and Its Chapters 1899-1977*, by Mrs. R.V. Love and Mrs. E.E. Bruno

- *MSSDAR 1982-1984 Pictorial Supplement to Historic Events of 1894-1977*, by Mrs. R.V. Love, Mrs. Sidney Groff and Miss Lorene Burks
- *The Anaconda Standard* newspaper, Anaconda Montana, "Beaverhead Rock to Have Marker," Sept. 1, 1921, pg. 12
- *The Anaconda Standard* newspaper, Anaconda Montana, "D.A.R. Places Marker - Lewis and Clark Trail," Sept. 7, 1921, pg. 9
- *The Mineral Independent* newspaper, Superior Montana, "Beaverhead Rock Famous Landmark," Sept. 22, 1921
- *The Tribune-Examiner* newspaper, Dillon Montana, "Beaverhead Rock Marker to be Placed," April 30, 1976
- *The Tribune-Examiner* newspaper, Dillon Montana, photo with caption, May 5, 1976
- *The Tribune-Examiner* newspaper, Dillon Montana, "Beaverhead Rock State Park Made Dream Come True," Sept. 3, 1980, pg. E-4

## Camp Fortunate

| | |
|---|---|
| **GPS coordinates** | n/a |
| **Commemorated** | An important Lewis and Clark Expedition campground where Sacajawea recognized her Shoshone chief brother, who provided horses and guides to cross the Continental Divide |
| **Site location** | 21 miles south of Dillon off I-15, one mile north of Armstead (now under Clark Canyon Dam waters) |
| **Installed** | September 12, 1937 |
| **Marker lost** | Due to theft and deterioration of subsequent wooden replacement signs |
| **Wording believed to be on original marker** | "The first white men in the Red Rock Valley were members of the Lewis and Clark Expedition. In August 1805, they camped for one week at a spot, on the east side of the river, which became known as Camp Fortunate. Sacajawea and Chief Cameahwait of the Shoshone Indian tribe recognized each other as brother and sister. Here, they were able to get horses to cross the divide to the west, making this camp a pivotal point to the success of the Lewis and Clark Expedition." |

# History

It was on a Sunday, September 12, 1937, that Beaverhead Chapter, NSDAR and the Beaverhead and Lemhi Mining Associations jointly dedicated a historical memorial park in front of an audience of hundreds of Montanans and Idahoans. The site was one mile north of the town of Armstead (now under Clark Canyon Dam waters), just below the confluence of the Red Rock River and Horse Prairie Creek. DAR member Laura Tolman Scott and Dr. Grace Raymond Hebard (the University of Wyoming) jointly gifted the land for the park; it was to be Laura Tolman Scott's last public appearance before her death. That summer, the State Highway Commission had constructed a park and roadside picnic area. The local *Dillon Examiner* newspaper reported that:

> *A basket lunch was served at 1 o'clock, preceding the program. Coffee, cream and suges were furnished by the Beaverhead Mining Association.*

DAR had long honored the spot, which was a Lewis and Clark campground used first on August 17 through 24, 1805, then again in 1806 by Captain Clark on his return from the Pacific Northwest. In 1916, Laura Tolman Scott, then a member of Silver Bow Chapter DAR, directed a pageant at the site.

Many historians say this site was the pivotal point of the Lewis and Clark Expedition's journey in that it could have ended there. Lewis and Clark had for months toiled up the Missouri River, portaged around the Great Falls, through the Gates of the Mountains and the Three Forks of the Missouri. They then chose the Jefferson River to continue their journey, but found their heavily laden canoes increasingly difficult to navigate. On August 17, 1805, they reached the "Two Forks of the Missouri" (Red Rock River and Horse Prairie Creek) where they found the river they had been following divided itself into two. It was journey's end for canoes and the most serious obstacle of the entire journey.

Fortunately, Meriwether Lewis and a band of Shoshone Indians led by Chief Cameawaite arrived. Indian guide Sacajawea, who had come up the Beaverhead River with Captain Clark, unexpectedly reunited with her birth brother, Chief Cameawaite, at the site. This "good fortune" led to the Corps of Discovery obtaining Indian horses and guides for the difficult trek over the Continental Divide to the Columbia. Thus, the name "Fortunate Camp"!

In the early 1960s when construction on the Clark Canyon Dam began, the DAR tablet was moved to a stone wall near Vista House overlooking the Lewis and Clark Expedition campsite. Vista House, built by the State of Montana, was later destroyed by vandals and the DAR bronze tablet stolen.

A replacement wooden marker on wood posts was placed by the U.S. Forest Service; it was rededicated by the Beaverhead Chapter in August 1968. That sign, which has since been lost due to deterioration, originally read:

> *The inspiration and effort of Mrs. Laura Tolman Scott and the Daughters of the American Revolution resulted in dedication of this area to the memory of Sacajawea—interpreter, guide, counselor of Lewis and Clark.*

Currently at the Clark Canyon Dam site, an informational sign set in a stone wall contains the following language:

*Fortunate Camp: This site was the pivotal point in the success of the Lewis and Clark Expedition. The party camped here in August 1805. They cached their boats and aided by the influence of Sacajawea obtained horses from her people, the Shoshone Indians. The great American epic of Lewis and Clark stands without parallel in the history of the opening of the west and the successful accomplishment was largely due to the guidance and loyalty of the Indian girl Sacajawea.*

*(by) Laura Tolman Scott*

SOURCES

- Historic monument records, Office of the Historian General, Wash. D.C.
- *Record of Tablets and Markers Placed by Montana DAR 1908-1947*, by Mrs. Fred E. May
- *State Centennial History, MSSDAR*, by Iris McKinney Gray, 1894-1994
- *Historical Sites Preserved and Markers Erected by MSSDAR and Its Chapters 1899-1977*, by Mrs. R.V. Love and Mrs. E.E. Bruno
- *MSSDAR 1982-1984 Pictorial Supplement to Historic Events of 1894-1977*, by Mrs. R.V. Love, Mrs. Sidney Groff and Miss Lorene Burks
- *The Dillon Examiner* newspaper, "Large Crowd Attends Formal Opening of Roadside Memorial," Sept. 15, 1937
- *The Montana Standard* newspaper, Butte Montana, "'Fortunate Camp' Dedicated at Dillon Was Most Important Site Along Route of Lewis and Clark," Sept. 19, 1937, pg. 62

# Lewis and Clark Trail Markers through Beaverhead County

The Beaverhead Chapter, NSDAR sponsored a reported 11 markers for the Lewis and Clark Expedition trail through Beaverhead County, based largely on the enthusiasm of Mrs. Laura Tolman Scott, chair of the Montana Society DAR Marking of Historic Spots and Old Trails Committee. During Mrs. Scott's 1920-1921 term as chapter regent, the chapter placed numerous metal road signs along the trail and at other historic sites in Beaverhead County.

In the summer of 1921, the chapter installed six metal markers on the Lewis and Clark Trail (and, possibly, at Bannack). While the number of signs is not in question (six), sources vary in naming which sites were marked. Two sources agree on these four:

1. Beaverhead Rock, where Sacajawea recognized "the land of my people"
2. Rattle Snake Cliff, named by Captain Lewis, Aug. 10, 1805
3. Sarvice Berrie Vallie, named by Lewis and Clark
4. Indian Head Mountain, on Horse Prairie

But then the two sources differ—each including two of this list:

1. Clark's Mountain, an August 16, 1805 campsite
2. Road Agent Rock, a danger spot near Bannack on the Virginia City road in the 1860s
3. Shoshone Cove, a flat valley where Captain Lewis sighted a lone Indian on horseback, the first seen in 139 days
4. Trail Creek, a tributary of the Horse Prairie, ascended by the Lewis and Clark Expedition

On September 5, 1921, the Beaverhead Chapter participated in a ceremony placing a "durable metal marker" furnished by the Beaverhead County commissioners at Beaverhead Rock, an Indian and pioneer landmark. Lewis and Clark sighted the landmark August 8, 1804.

Later, on September 4, 1922, the chapter placed markers at Lemhi Pass and at the spring the Lewis and Clark Expedition called "The Distant Fountain of the Missouri." One source reported that "a marker was also placed at "the Buttes."

Three more metal markers were dedicated on October 19, 1922, during the 19th State DAR Conference. These were:

1. Selway Bridge north of Dillon

2. Beaverhead Bridge, a mile southwest of Dillon
3. The third metal marker's site is unclear. One historical account says "Van Camps," two others say "Oregon Short Line depot lawn at Dillon" ("centre of the station square")

On August 27, 1923, the chapter placed two more metal markers:

1. At "Boiling Springs" in the Big Hole Basin which Captain Clark discovered on his return journey from the Pacific Northwest in 1806
2. Jackson, Montana "on the main road"

While little is known about most of the marker dedications, a *Butte Miner* newspaper article dated September 2, 1923, told about the "Boiling Springs" marker ceremonies in which the DAR marker was presented to the residents of the Big Hole basin:

> *Two hundred fifty persons from Wisdom, Jackson, Elkhorn Springs, Dillon and other points joined in the picnic luncheon spread under the trees of the meadow, after which all went to the community hall, where a historical program of more than usual merit was given. … The program was "America"; "Washington's prayer," Mrs. Clark Anderson, Dillon; D.A.R. salute to the flag, address, Mrs. E. Broox Martin, Bozeman, state regent D.A.R.; piano solo, Mrs. Kay Wiley, Wisdom; "This Day in History," G.R. Squires, Wisdom; "Lewis and Clark in Beaverhead County," F.H. (Frank) Garver, Dillon; vocal solo, Mrs. Herbert Armitage, Wisdom; "The Composition of the Lewis and Clark Party," Dr. Grace Raymond Hebard, Laramie, Wyo.; presentation of the marker, Mrs. Laura Tolman Scott, Armstead.*

The next year, on August 23, 1924, the chapter placed nine more metal markers at Bannack, the first territorial capitol of Montana. These marked the first legislative hall, the first governor's residence

(Gov. Sidney Edgerton), the first school, the first jail, Skinner's Saloon, Henry Plummer's grave, and "other historic sites."

The next marker was placed on August 24, 1926, at Anderson Bridge across the Beaverhead River marking the "Three Thousand Mile Island" referred to in Lewis and Clark's records. Captain Lewis estimated that to be the distance from St. Louis. The island was on the Anderson Ranch, six miles north of Dillon, the site of a DAR picnic. Mrs. Laura Tolman Scott gave the history of the island and Miss Jean Bishop "related later historical incidents of the community, including those of the famous Stone Crossing and of the story of the cows that were locked in the milk house."

Next, on October 22, 1927, the Beaverhead Chapter placed a metal marker at "Clark's Lookout," where Clark took observations and recorded them in his diary on August 13, 1805. This site is one mile north of Dillon on old Highway 91 and is now a Montana State Park.

SOURCES
- Historic monument records, Office of the Historian General, Wash. D.C.
- *Record of Tablets and Markers Placed by Montana DAR 1908-1947*, by Mrs. Fred E. May (This is the source mentioned in the 1921 and Sept. 1922 marker placements.)
- *State Centennial History, MSSDAR*, by Iris McKinney Gray, 1894-1994
- *DAR Magazine*, "Montana State Conference," Feb. 1923, pg. 96
- *The Anaconda Standard* newspaper, Anaconda Montana, "Beaverhead Rock to Have Marker," Sept. 1, 1921, pg. 12
- *The Butte Miner* newspaper, Butte Montana, "Historical Celebration of National Interest Held at Lemhi Pass," Sept. 10, 1922, pg. 39
- *The Dillon Tribune* newspaper, Dillon Montana, "D.A.R. Convention Held Here," Oct. 20, 1922
- *The Butte Miner* newspaper, Butte Montana, "Trail of Lewis and Clark is Traced by D.A.R. of Dillon," Sept. 2, 1923, pg. 7
- *The Dillon Examiner* newspaper, Dillon Montana, "Twelfth Annual Picnic Held by D.A.R. at the Anderson Ranch," Aug. 25, 1926, pg. 1
- *The Anaconda Standard* newspaper, Anaconda Montana, "Will Place Marker Near Lover's Leap," Oct. 19, 1927, pg. 8

# Lewis and Clark Trail Markers - Bear Island to Grand Falls

Little is known about these markers except that they were a shared expense between the Black Eagle Chapter, NSDAR and Boy Scouts. The two organizations placed five bronze markers between White Bear Island and "Grand Falls" on the Missouri River to commemorate the Lewis and Clark Trail. The markers were placed wherever a highway crossed the trail.

SOURCE
- Historic monument records, Office of the Historian General, Washington D.C.

# Madison River Toll Bridge and Tipi Rings

| | |
|---|---|
| **GPS coordinates** | n/a |
| **Commemorated** | The Madison River toll bridge and Indian tipi rings that marked the route of countless settlers and miners and by Indians as campgrounds |
| **Site location** | West of Bozeman at the Madison River Bridge, Montana Highway 84, Norris |
| **Installed** | November 1964 and again in 1974 |
| **Marker lost** | Due to deterioration of wooden signs |
| **Wording** | "A toll bridge was in use from 1870 to 1880. Across it rolled the wagons and miners, six-horse stage coaches, and gold shipments from the rich mines in this region. Deep ruts on both banks once marked this important pioneer road. This area was also a popular Indian campsite. Rock circles called 'Teepee Rings' can be seen nearby. Daughters of the American Revolution Mount Hyalite Chapter and Bureau of Land Management." |

# History

This was Mount Hyalite Chapter, NSDAR's third historic marker. In 1964 and again in 1974, the chapter installed a wooden marker on two posts at the Madison Toll Bridge site to commemorate an important pioneer road as well as a popular Indian campsite.

The toll bridge was used by settlers and miners, stage coaches, and for shipping gold. The Madison River Bridge was near the present-day ghost town of Red Bluff and was used from 1870 to 1888 by miners who transported gold on this old Indian trail between Virginia City and Helena. The area was also used by camping Indians—"teepee rings" can be seen nearby (stone circles).

In 1870, Milton and Robert Canaday invested $400 in the bridge and sold it eight years later to Paul D. Hayward for the same amount. Over time, the bridge deteriorated and on May 18, 1882, the local paper reported,

> *On Thursday of last week as a freighter was crossing the Madison bridge he heard an ominous cracking of timber, and whipping up his team, succeeded in getting over just as one span of the bridge gave way.*

The bridge was replaced and two years later, Madison County bought it, making it a free thoroughfare after nearly 20 years. The original bridge washed away in the late 1880s and only the pilings and approach ramps remain today.

The DAR markers are no longer there. A new bridge and a park are now a little further from the original bridge site. Signage placed by the Bureau of Land Management explains the former existence of the bridge and its importance to early settlers and commerce.

**SOURCES**

- Historic monument records, Office of the Historian General, Washington D.C.
- *State Centennial History, MSSDAR*, by Iris McKinney Gray, Vol. V 1894-1994 (Note: initial installation date mistakenly shown as 1968 in this source.)
- *Historical Sites Preserved and Markers Erected by MSSDAR and Its Chapters 1899-1977*, by Mrs. R.V. Love and Mrs. E.E. Bruno
- *MSSDAR 1982-1984 Pictorial Supplement to Historic Events of 1894-1977*, by Mrs. R.V. Love, Mrs. Sidney Groff and Miss Lorene Burks
- Bureau of Land Management signage at Madison River Bridge pullout

# 35. OTHER DAR COMMEMORATIONS

Some of the historic preservation work of the Montana State Society DAR does not fit into the category of "markers" or "monuments," nor are some located in Montana. Regardless, their history is important, so these six "other commemorations" are listed in this chapter in order by year, oldest to newest.

## Montana Copper Spade

| | |
|---|---|
| **GPS coordinates** | 38.89421852 \| -77.04031601 |
| **Commemorated** | The building of DAR Memorial Continental Hall and construction of Constitution Hall |
| **Site location** | Americana Room at DAR headquarters in Washington D.C. |
| **Donated** | October 11, 1902 |

### History

Donated on October 11, 1902, for the ground-breaking ceremonies for DAR Memorial Continental Hall's construction and used again for

DAR Constitution Hall in 1926, the Montana Copper Spade continues to be used for special events yet today.

The design of the spade is credited to Organizing (first) Regent of the Silver Bow Chapter, NSDAR Mrs. Jennie Stilwell Tallant, known as the "Grand Dame" of Montana Daughters for her large tea parties and musicales and for hosting numerous DAR meetings. For this Montana gift, she selected Montana copper for the blade and wood from a tree on the Lewis and Clark Trail in Montana for the handle. Blue and white ribbons from the Mary Washington Colonial Chapter of New York City were tied to the spade's handle as a symbol of recognition of all sections of the country participating in the memorable event.

Montana DAR history records suggest that Organizing Regent of the Yellowstone Park Chapter, NSDAR, Mrs. Hugh J. (Georgiana Cole) Miller was "instrumental in securing the copper from the Anaconda Mining Company for the spade…."

It was on the 12th anniversary of the founding of the National Society of the Daughters of the American Revolution, in a "blinding afternoon rainstorm" on October 11, 1902, that DAR President General Mrs. Charles Fairbanks and number of other members broke ground for the DAR Memorial Continental Hall to be built in the memory of the men and women who struggled against the tyranny of Great Britain. The event drew several hundred Sons and Daughters of the American Revolution, who gathered under a tent for the program. Mrs. Fairbanks is quoted as having said, "We go forth in the rain to our duty but our ancestors did more during the Revolution."

At the conclusion of her speech, Mrs. Fairbanks, accompanied by Mrs. Mary S. Lockwood, one of the DAR's founders:

*... stepped into the lot in front of the tent, and Mrs. Lockwood spaded a jar full of earth from the spot on which the new building is to stand. She used a copper spade, presented by the Montana Chapter of the Daughters of the American Revolution. The blade is of copper from Montana mines, and the handle is of wood cut from the path, the Virginians, Lewis and Clark trod when they first explored what is now the State of Montana. The handle is adorned with Montana gold and silver and set with sapphires. It was decorated with ribbons (the blue and white ribbons are still attached) given by the Mary Washington Colonial Chapter, of New York City. All sections of this vast land were thus recognized in this symbolic spade.*

*The pot of earth was carried into the tent, and Mrs. Lockwood planted thirteen osage orange seeds in it, in commemoration of the thirteen original colonies, explaining that as the osage plants grow sprouts will be removed and given to various state and local branches of the organization.*

The article quoted above concluded with a poem written to honor the beginning of the new building by Montana DAR member Ella Wheeler Wilcox titled, "The Continental Hall." The last paragraph of her poem says:

> *And though we stand as "Daughters"*
> *Of men whom duty drove*
> *Through massacres and slaughters*
> *Where death and hatred throve,*
> *Yet our chief pride is knowing,*
> *That in our veins is flowing*
> *The motherhood of love.*

The spade was once again used to break ground for the DAR Constitution Hall in 1926, but as years passed, the spade faded from sight. On April 20, 1978, after considerable searching, NSDAR Museum Curator Mr. Cato found Montana's famous spade in a grounds committee closet. The DAR Museum does not contain artifacts of later than a 1830 origin, so the spade could not be placed there. Thus, the spade was moved to the NSDAR Library balcony, then more recently moved to the Americana Room of the NSDAR Archives at DAR national headquarters.

In 1979, Montana State Regent Mrs. Alta (Orrion) Pilon chose for her project to provide a suitable case for displaying the Montana spade. Mrs. Pilon felt, because of its great historic value, the spade should have a proper display case. Due to her work, the spade is now housed in a case made of Montana pine, lined with DAR blue velvet, and sitting on a hand-rubbed base made of a Montana juniper root. State Regent Mrs. Pilon presented this case to President General Mrs. George Bayliss of the National Society at the 1979 Montana State Conference in Billings. A plaque on the spade's case says, "Gift of Montana Society Daughters of the American Revolution 1929-1980, Mrs. Alta Pilon, Regent."

*Montana Copper Spade in Americana Room*

Since the spade has been put on public display, it has been used several times to plant shrubs or trees at DAR headquarters and at Mount Vernon for memorial services.

SOURCES

- Historic monument records, Office of the Historian General, Wash. D.C.
- *State Centennial History, MSSDAR*, by Iris McKinney Gray, Vol. V 1894-1994
- *MSSDAR 1982-1984 Pictorial Supplement to Historic Events of 1894-1977*, by Mrs. R.V. Love, Mrs. Sidney Groff and Miss Lorene Burks
- "Breaks Ground Memorial Continental Hall," information supplied by Mrs. Hazel Fuller Kreinheder, Historical Research NSDAR, circa 1970s
- *American Monthly Magazine* (DAR), "The Continental Hall, Daughters of the American Revolution," Nov. 1902, pps. 353-360
- *Great Falls Tribune* newspaper, Great Falls Montana, "Furnished the Spade," Oct. 12, 1902, pg. 4

# The Washington Elm

| | |
|---|---|
| **GPS coordinates** | n/a |
| **Commemorated** | George Washington's Bicentennial |
| **Site location** | State capitol grounds, Helena |
| **Installed** | May 10, 1932 |

## HISTORY

It was on a Tuesday, May 10, 1932, that the Oro Fino Chapter, NSDAR conducted a ceremony dedicating a newly-planted young elm tree donated by the DAR of Maryland. The elm was called by the local paper a "grandchild" of the famous Washington Elm in Cambridge, Massachusetts. (While never verified, many believe that it was under the Washington Elm that George Washington stood when he accepted command of the Continental Army in the Revolutionary War in 1775.)

The ceremony started with bugle calls of "Assemble" and "Attention," then "America" by the local high school glee club and band. Governor John E. Erickson accepted the tree on behalf of the state of Montana and DAR members deposited soil around the base of the tree. The local newspaper detailed the origin of each deposit:

*Mrs. A.K. Prescott, chapter member of Oro Fino chapter, placed soil from Wakefield, Virginia, the birthplace of Washington; Mrs. J. E. Erickson, soil from the home of Mary-Ball Washington at Fredericksburg, Va.; Mrs. C.A. Rasmusson, soil from Cambridge, Mass., where the original elm stood; Mrs. G.A. Willett, soil around the tree from Independence Square, Philadelphia, and Mrs. C.C. Warn of Billings deposited a quantity of soil from Annapolis, Md., the birthplace of the small elm tree which now stands on the capitol grounds.*

A Montana Historical Society Research Center Photograph Archives picture of the event (#957-660) shows 27 dignitaries lined up behind the small tree with a U.S. flag flying in the background. The site appears to be close to the capitol building on its northwest side.

**SOURCE**
- *The Independent-Record* newspaper, Helena Montana, "Washington Elm Dedicated on State Capitol Grounds," May 11, 1932, pg. 5

# Sacajawea Recreation Area, Lemhi Pass

| | |
|---|---|
| **GPS coordinates** | 44.97018593 | -113.44351774 |
| **Commemorated** | Sacajawea, Shoshone Indian Guide for the Lewis & Clark Expedition |
| **Site location** | Continental Divide at Lemhi Pass, between Salmon, Idaho and Grant, Montana |
| **Dedicated** | *Original:* August 14, 1932 |
| | *Rededication:* August 1968 |
| **Marker** | This was not a DAR marker |
| **USFS sign** | *Original:* No sign erected |
| | *1968 Rededication:* U.S. Forest Service sign- "The inspiration and effort of Mrs. Laura Tolman Scott and the Daughters of the American Revolution resulted in dedication of this area to the memory of Sacajawea—interpreter, guide, counselor of Lewis and Clark." |

## HISTORY

On August 14, 1932, almost 500 people from both Montana and Idaho assembled for the dedication of Sacajawea National Monument, a new recreational area established by the federal government in memory of the courageous Shoshone Indian guide for the Lewis and Clark Expedition. It was at the Lemhi Pass summit (7,373 feet above sea level) that Captain Meriwether Lewis and three of his men first saw the Pacific slope on August 12, 1805; Captain William A. Clark and 11 others reached the site a few days afterwards, on August 19.

In 1932, after persistent lobbying organized by Laura Tolman Scott of the DAR, the U.S. Secretary of Agriculture established the Sacajawea Recreation Division of the Salmon and Beaverhead National Forests at Lemhi Pass, honoring Sacajawea who served with her husband Toussaint Charbonneau as an interpreter and guide for the Lewis and Clark Expedition. The recreational area consisted of 140 acres on both sides of the state line.

The dedication was a joint effort by the Beaverhead Chapter, NSDAR, the Beaverhead and Lemhi Mining Associations, and the National Forest Service. The chair of the event, B. J. Metlen, Vice President of the Beaverhead Mining Association, introduced speakers Archdeacon Nash (Coeur d'Alene, Idaho), Professor O.A. Dingman of the Montana School of Mines (Butte), and Beaverhead National Forest Supervisor Alva A. Simpson. Chairman Metlen also introduced R.F. Hammat, Assistant Regional Forester (Missoula) who stated:

*There were many heroes in this band of intrepid explorers; there was but one heroine. Denied in life–and after–that recognition which was due her, it is fitting that we meet here today to dedicate this spot in honor of that heroine.*

Another speaker, Dr. Grace Raymond Hebard, faculty of University of Wyoming and a widely-recognized authority on Western history, told of Sacajawea's part of the "Great Expedition of Exploration." Mrs. J.W. Scott (Laura Tolman Scott, Armstead, Montana), National District Chair of Historic Sites for the DAR, was recognized for her years-long efforts to secure the famous spot's designation as a national monument.

And, of course, there was music—the crowd sang "America the Beautiful" at the beginning and "All People That on Earth Do Dwell" at the conclusion of the monument's dedication.

In 1940, a one-mile wildflower trail was built at the Sacajawea Memorial Area to honor Laura Tolman Scott, who was a passionate wildflower admirer and collector. (Some of her wildflower collection is on display in the Beaverhead County Museum in Dillon.) The wildflower trail showcases the variety of Rocky Mountain plant communities, which are at their peak in June and July.

In 1960, the area was designated a National Historic Landmark, and in 1991, landmark boundaries were established encompassing 480 acres. Under the National Trails System Act of 1968, the Continental Divide National Scenic Trail was authorized, and ten years later, the Lewis and Clark National Historic Trail was also designated by Congress.

Currently, the area has picnic tables and fire rings and interpretive signs along Lemhi Pass Trail, Sacajawea Memorial Area, and along Westward View trail.

In August of 1968, Montana State Society DAR and the Beaverhead Chapter held rededication ceremonies of Sacajawea Park and also dedicated three wooden markers: Sacajawea Historical Area, An Advanced Party, and Sacajawea Park. The U.S. Forest Service provided the wooden signs, which are no longer on the site. Among prominent people at the rededication ceremony were G. Edward (Gus) Budde, the St. Louis representative of the Lewis and Clark Trail Heritage Foundation; Montana State Regent Mrs. Walter Mondale of Lewistown; and speaker Hal Stearns, Director of the Historical Society of Salmon, Idaho. Event Chair Mrs. Elfreda (J. Fred) Woodside, Beaverhead Chapter DAR, led the rededication.

SOURCES
- Historic monument records, Office of the Historian General, Wash. D.C.
- *Historical Sites Preserved and Markers Erected by MSSDAR and Its Chapters, 1899-1977*, by Mrs. R.V. Love and Mrs. E.E. Bruno

- *MSSDAR 1982-1984 Pictorial Supplement to Historic Events of 1894-1977*, by Mrs. R.V. Love, Mrs. Sidney Groff and Miss Lorene Burks
- *The Independent Record* newspaper, Helena Montana, "National Monument in Lemhi Pass to be Opened Today," Aug. 14, 1932, pg. 16
- *The Dillon Examiner* newspaper, Dillon Montana, "National Monument is Dedicated Last Sunday," Aug. 17, 1932
- USDA Forest Service Beaverhead-Deerlodge and Salmon-Challis National Forests Lemhi Pass National Historic Landmark. Found at https://www.fs.usda.gov/Internet/FSE_DOCUMENTS/stelprdb5052332.pdf

*Current view of Lemhi Pass area (elevation 7,373 feet)*

# George Washington Bicentennial DAR Tree

**GPS coordinates**   n/a
**Commemorated**   George Washington's Bicentennial
**Site location**   Pioneer Park, Billings (tree has since died)
**Installed**   September 30, 1932

## HISTORY

During the September 30, 1932, bicentennial celebration of the birth of George Washington, the Billings Washington Bicentennial Committee, led by D.L. Chambers, presented 13 cedar trees planted in Pioneer Park. The tree saplings came from a pasture in Ferry Farm, the boyhood home of George Washington on the Rappahannock River opposite Fredericksburg, Virginia. The trees represented the 13 original colonies. They were shipped to Billings and planted in a semi-circle at Pioneer Park.

At the 11:30 a.m. ceremony, Mayor F.L. Tilton presented the trees to the 13 sponsoring organizations, which included the Shining Mountain Chapter NSDAR, Kiwanis Club, Lions Club, Rotary Club, Billings Commercial Club, Billings Garden Club, Masonic organizations, American Legion Auxiliary, Veterans of Foreign Wars Auxiliary, Knights of Columbus, YMCA, and DeMolay and DeMolay alumni.

The seventh tree numbering from the west was the DAR tree.

The history of this park is also interesting. In 1918, the city had purchased 35 acres northwest of the city for use as a city park. Rather than name it after one of Billings' early pioneers, the community named its new park for all of them. In the summer of 1921, the Billings parks board hired Dorothy M. Gray (her later married name was Johnson) to draft plans for the new park. Not only was it unique to see landscape architects in the West, it was especially rare to see a woman landscape architect.

Gray's original design included several monuments and other tributes to veterans, and features like a lily pond, a lake, and tennis courts. While a number of trees were planted in the decade following Gray's original work, funding shortfalls prevented much of her design from being constructed until after the park's 1932 dedication.

The park was dedicated in July 1932 as part of the city's semi-centennial. DAR planned a memorial walk for veterans who died during World War I. Currently, all that remains of that walk are a pair of stone columns on Grand Avenue on the Senior High School campus.

SOURCES

- Historic monument records, Office of the Historian General, Wash. D.C.
- *Historical Sites Preserved and Markers Erected by MSSDAR and Its Chapters 1899-1977,* by Mrs. R.V. Love and Mrs. E.E. Bruno
- *The Billings Gazette* newspaper, Billings Montana, "Tree Dedication Ceremonies Set," Sept. 30, 1932

## First State Regent

| | |
|---|---|
| **GPS coordinates** | n/a |
| **Commemorates** | Mary DeVeny Wasson, Montana's first state regent |
| **Site location** | Woodlawn Cemetery, New York State |
| **Installed** | April 25, 1977 |
| **Marker wording** | "Mary DeVeny Wasson (Mrs. Edmund A.), First State Regent Montana Society NSDAR, 1894-1899, placed by Montana State Society NSDAR April 25, 1977" |

# History

The dedication of a bronze plaque mounted on a granite base at the grave of Montana's first state regent, Mary DeVeny (Mrs. Edmund A.) Wasson took place on April 25, 1977, at 2:00 p.m. under sunny skies. DAR members from two states gathered at historic Woodlawn Cemetery in Bronx County, New York, for the event.

Over 80 years before, on May 9, 1894, DAR's National Board of Management had appointed Mrs. Wasson to be Montana state regent and gave her the assignment to organize a chapter in Montana. But, due to multiple family tragedies, she in turn appointed Mrs. Walter S. (Jennie Stilwell) Tallant of Butte to serve as organizing regent for a chapter in Butte (the Silver Bow Chapter, chartered on December 21, 1897).

Mrs. Wasson continued as Montana state regent until 1899. Then in 1900, she and her family moved to Newark, New Jersey. She remained a DAR member of the Silver Bow Chapter for 56 years until her death at age 93 in New York City on June 3, 1953.

After years of searching by Montana State Regent Mrs. G.P. (Berniece Metlen) Palmer, then later by Miss E. Lorene Burks and Mrs. R.V. Love, Mrs. Wasson's grave was finally located in New York City's Woodlawn Cemetery. Mrs. Wasson and her husband Edmund had been laid to rest in a plot marked only by a granite Celtic cross about eight feet high, without inscription. Mrs. Wasson's son (R. Gordon Wasson) gave permission to DAR to place a marker on her grave to commemorate Mary DeVeny Wasson as the first State Regent of the Montana State Society DAR.

It was a "reverent ceremony" in 1977 in which participated four New York DAR members–New York State Director Districts I and II Mrs. Herbert P. Poole, Battle Pass Chapter Regent Miss Ethel E. Probst, New Netherland Chapter Regent Mrs. Royal M. Bechwith, and New York City Chapter Regent Mrs. Morris Young. Also attending were Mr. R. Gordon Wasson of Danbury, Connecticut (Mrs. Wasson's only surviving son) and Mr. Royal Bechwith.

The Montana delegation to the ceremony were Montana State Regent Miss E. Lorene Burks (presiding), Montana State Secretary Mrs. Thomas Murray, Past Vice President General Miss Marjorie Stevenson, Shining Mountain Chapter Regent Mrs. Jess T. Schwidde, past Shining Mountain Chapter Regent Mrs. Eugene E. Taber, and Julia Hancock Chapter Regent Mrs. Henry McVey.

Mrs. Jess T. Schwidde opened the ceremony, saying:

*Remember the past is conserving strength for the future. As we look at history, we know that we need today–not a show of greatness, not a parade of power, not a recital of our capacities–but more and more a spirit of fervent gratitude; and again and again, a consecration of our own selves to the achievement of great ideals. We are the heirs of high endeavor; ere long we too shall belong to the past. Let us now with quiet and grateful hearts remember before God the dearly beloved dead. They have left our earthly companionship but still they live within our hearts. The remembrance of them is dear and blessed.*

After State Regent Miss E. Lorene Burks unveiled the bronze plaque, Mrs. Herbert P. Poole, on behalf of the New York State Society DAR, next spoke, saying,

*We thank Thee, Lord, for this far-sighted State Regent whose vision was the beginning of the Montana State Society, Daughters of the American Revolution. We thank Thee for the good foundations she laid and for our inheritance of dreams and aspirations. Bless the enlarging vision which has come through the years which has let us into material and spiritual growth. Make us an ever increasing force for good. Accept our service to our generation and strengthen us in all that is worthwhile. For they are not dead who live in hearts they leave behind, in those whom they have blessed they live a life again.*

Mary DeVeny Wasson's son gave a personal tribute to his mother, followed by Mrs. Murray placing a sheaf of red roses on the plaque.

### Sources

- *State History Montana Society Daughters of the American Revolution 1970-80*, author unknown
- *State Centennial History, MSSDAR*, by Iris McKinney Gray, 1894-1994
- *Historical Sites Preserved and Markers Erected by MSSDAR and Its Chapters 1899-1977*, by Mrs. R.V. Love and Mrs. E.E. Bruno
- Unlabeled one-page document with photos

## DAR-SAR 125th Anniversary Tree

| | |
|---|---|
| **GPS coordinates** | 46.5883001977 \| -112.0139907673 |
| **Commemorated** | Montana DAR and SAR's 125th Anniversary |
| **Site location** | 6th Avenue and Sanders Street, Helena |
| **Marker wording** | "Montana State Society Daughters of the American Revolution Montana Society Sons of the American Revolution 125th Anniversary 1894 – 2019" |
| **Installed** | April 25, 2019 |

# History

MSSDAR's 2019 State Conference, held April 25-27, celebrated the 125th Anniversary of DAR's founding in Montana. Since the Montana SAR was also founded in Montana in 1894, the two organizations held several joint state events along with each organization's separate state conferences. To commemorate the occasion, DAR and SAR shared the $500 cost of placing a Tatarian maple tree on the State Capitol grounds next to a plaque inset in concrete.

A crowd of about 100 DAR and SAR members attended the 4:15 pm ceremony on April 25. The dedication began with a SAR Color Guard made up of four Montana State Society SAR members: Steve Armstrong (drummer, MTSSAR Vice President and Glacier Chapter SAR), Keith Kramlick (Vice President, Guardian Chapter SAR), Doug Fraser (Guardian Chapter SAR), and T.C. Richardson (MTSSAR Chaplain and Liberty Tree Chapter SAR). Local Helena High School bugler, Kennedy Black, played "Assembly." State Chaplain Janice S. Hand gave the invocation. MSSDAR State Regent Jane Lee Hamman gave the welcome for DAR and MTSSAR State President Larry Mylnechuk gave the welcome for SAR.

The tree chosen for the site was a Tatarian maple because its leaves turn the brightest red of any tree available of those allowable for planting at the State Capitol complex. Since red in the U.S. Flag symbolizes the strength, courage and valor of American Patriots, this species of tree was selected to perpetuate the memory and spirit of our Patriots during the 125th Anniversary.

Among State Regent Hamman's comments were these:

*Historically, our lineage societies have planted trees since we were founded. Planting trees is deemed to be a good way to honor the Patriots in our family trees, as well as contribute to the beauty and health of our communities. Trees propagated from those planted by George Washington and Thomas Jefferson abound across the land. During World War I, Oro Fino Chapter partnered with SAR to purchase and plant Colorado blue spruce trees in Helena's new city parks. In 1926, our Society marked the 150th anniversary of the American Revolution by contributing funds to help plant 13 trees, one for each Colony, in Independence Park in Philadelphia. In May 1932, DAR and SAR officers gathered to plant a Washington Elm tree right next to the Montana capitol. In 2017, NSDAR provided $220,000 for the planting of 76 trees in Independence Park to prepare for our nation's Semiquincentennial which will begin in 2026, and currently we are planting 250 trees along a Pathway of Patriots to honor the memory and perpetuate the spirit of the men and women who achieved American Independence. So, for our 125$^{th}$ Anniversary in Montana, it is fitting that we plant this attractive Tatarian maple for the next generation.*

After members of both organizations placed shovels-full of soil around the newly-planted tree, concluding the tree-planting ceremony, the SAR Color Guard led the crowd in a walk to the Montana Liberty Bell at the corner of Roberts Street and 5$^{th}$ Avenue. There, MSSDAR State Regent Jane Lee Hamman gave the history of Montana's Liberty Bell, followed by MTSSAR President Larry Mylnechuk who gave the commemoration and rededication of the bell.

SOURCES
- Book author Janice S. Hand attended and participated in this ceremony.
- *The Helena Independent Record* newspaper, Helena Montana, "Daughters and Sons of American Revolution Plant Tree at Capitol," May 10, 2019

# Index

10th U.S. Cavalry, **105**
11th Infantry, **90**
13th Infantry, **17**
1st U.S. Cavalry, **90**
24th Infantry, **105**
25th Infantry, **105**
2nd U.S. Cavalry, **90, 98**
5th U.S. Cavalry, **98**
7th Infantry, **114, 161**
7th U.S. Cavalry, **98**
Abrams, Mrs. Jack, **82**
Abrams, Shirley Case, **82**
Adams, J.Q., **154**
Adams, Mrs. F.W., **6**
Albright, R.E., **38, 42, 58**
Allen, Mrs. Harry, **6**
Allen, W.R., **43**
American Fur Company, **64, 65**
An Advanced Party, **189**
Anaconda Copper Mining Company, **v, 11, 16, 28, 41, 46, 52, 59, 81, 90, 94, 98, 104, 108, 114, 120, 134, 160, 166, 182**
ACM, **v, vi**
Anderson Bridge, **177**
Anderson, Mrs. A.L., **167**
Anderson, Mrs. Clark, **176**
Argenta, **38**
Armitage, Mrs. Herbert, **176**
Armstead, **51, 52, 172**

Armstrong, Steve, **196**
Arnold, John, **94**
Ashcraft, Mr. and Mrs. Norman, **168**
Assiniboine Indians, **72, 104**
Austin, Mrs. G.R., **72**
Babcock, Governor Tim, **168**
Bannack, **vi, viii, ix, 38, 43, 45, 46, 175, 176**
Bannock Indians, **46**
Barker, Butterworth, **28, 29**
Barretts Station, **57**
Baucus, Senator Max, **150**
Bayliss, Mrs. George, **184**
Beaverhead Bridge, **176**
Beaverhead Rock, **vi, vii, ix, 43, 165, 166, 167, 175**, See Point of Rocks
Bechwith, Mr. Royal, **194**
Bechwith, Mrs. Royal M., **194**
Becker, Mrs. Ervin, **2**
Becker, Mrs. William A. (Florence), **58**
Bell, Wilda, **29**
Berg, Sidney and Arthur, **162**
Berry, Mrs. George H., **82**
Billings, **xii, 1, 2, 5, 9, 191**
Bishop, John, **167**
Bishop, Miss Jean, **166, 177**
Bishop, Mrs. John F., **38**

Blackfeet Indians, **64, 86, 104**
Boiling Springs, **176**
Boll, Olive, **29**
Bovee, Orpha Zilpha Parke, 75
Bowles, John J., **114, 120**
Boy Scouts, **156, 178**
Bozeman, **xii, 15, 16, 19, 154, 178**
Bradley, Captain James, **17**
Brainard, Brigadier General David L., **90**
Brannon, Mrs. M.A., **108**
Brenner, State Sen. J.S., **166**
Brigham, C.A., **53**
Brosseau, Mrs. Grace Lincoln Hall, **28**
Brown, Helen, **29**
Brown, Jack, **170**
Browne, Antoinette Van Hook, **34, 63**
Browne, Mrs. David G. (Antoinette Van Hook), **66**
Bruno, Mrs. E.E., **xi**
Budd, Ralph, **82**
Budde, G. Edward (Gus), **189**
Buell, Lieutenant Colonel G.P., **90**
Burks, Miss E. Lorene, **xi, 126, 193, 194**
Butte, **xii, 23, 24, 25, 27, 33, 154**
Caldwell, Mrs. Verne D., **134, 160**
Callaway, Chief Justice L.L., **108**

Camp Fortunate, **vii, ix, 58, 164, 168, 171**
Canaday, Milton and Robert, **179**
Cavanaugh, James M., **116**
Chambers, D.L., **191**
Cheyenne, **94**
Chicago, Milwaukee, St. Paul and Pacific Railroad, **153, 154**
Chief Joseph, **17, 97, 99, 115, 144, 161**
Chinook, **97**
Clack, Mrs. Earl, **104**
Clapp, Charles H., **134**
Clark Canyon Dam, **51, 172**
Clark Carlson-Thompson, **83**
Clark, Senator W.A., **52, 54, 154**
Clark's Lookout, **177**
Clark's Mountain, **175**
Coleman, Mrs. Laura, **72**
Collins, John, **43**
Condon, Eliza A. Sturtevant, **63, 66**
Cooke, Mrs. Anthony W., **2**
Cooney, Governor Frank H., **58**
Cornelius, Mrs. Garrett, **2**
Cree, **104**
Crippen, Gertrude, **6**
Crook, Brigadier General George, **94**
Crow, **94**
Crow Agency, **91**
Culbertson, Alexander, **65**

Custer, General George Armstrong, **17, 89, 90**
DAR Real Daughter, **75, 147**
Davidson, Gene, **86**
Davidson, Mrs. M.P., **16**
Davis, Dr. Sheldon E., **43**
Deadwood Crossing, **140**
Delsigne, Barbara, **149**
DeSmet, Father, **58**
Dilavou, Mrs. R.C., **11, 94**
Dilavou, R.C., **i, 11**
Dillon, **vii, ix, xii, 37, 41, 42, 45, 51, 57, 59, 171, 175, 189**
Dingman, O.A., **188**
Dixon, Governor Joseph N., **160**
Duer, Mr. and Mrs. Charles E., **66**
Durfee, Commander E.H., **72**
Eastman, Sarah E., **66**
Eatinger, Mrs. Ramon, **126**
Edgerton, Gov. Sidney, **47, 177**
Elk Park, **82, 135**
Ellis, Colonel Augustus Van Horn, **17**
Erickson, Governor John E., **46, 108, 111, 186**
Erickson, Mrs. J. E., **186**
Fairbanks, Mrs. Charles, **182**
Farrell, Marta, **150**
Farrington, Jane, **29**
Farwell, Abel, **72**
Finnegan, Patrick, **156**
Foote, Don C., **12**
Fort Baker, **160**
Fort Benton, **viii, x, xii, 58, 63, 65, 72, 115**
Fort Keogh, **140, 143**
Fort Logan, **159**
Fort Meade, **140**
Fort Peck, **71**
Fox, William, **2**
Fraser, Doug, **196**
Gaddis, Charles, **160, 162**
Gaddis, Judge Williams, **162**
Garver, Frank, **176**
Garver, Frank H., **167**
Genovese, Cheryl A., **i, 206**
Gibbons, General, **17**
Gibson, Miss Kathy, **155**
Gibson, Mrs. A. J., **135**
Glasgow, **xii, 71**
Glasgow, Robert, **2**
Glen, **38**
Glendive, **xii, 75, 77, 78, 148**
Grand Falls, **178**
Grant, General Ulysses S., **15, 16**
Gray, Dorothy M., **191**
Gray, Hugh, **59**
Gray, Iris McKinney, **xi**
Great Falls, **xii, 53, 81, 82, 85**
Great Northern Railway, **82**
Griswold, Mr. John M., **134**
Groff, Shirley, **xi, 29, 68**
Gros Ventre, **104**

Grover & Leuchars, **82**
Hamilton, Jean, **20**
Hamman, Jane Lee, **xi**, **196**
Hammat, R.F., **188**
Hancock, Major General Winfield Scott, **160**
Hand, Janice S., **i**, **196**, **206**
Hardin, **xii**, **89**, **91**, **93**
Harwood, Ben, **94**
Haskell, Mrs. Henri J. (Ella Knowles), **34**
Havre, **xii**, **65**, **103**
Hayes, President Rutherford B., **89**, **90**
Hayward, Paul D., **179**
Hazelbaker, Sen. Frank, **170**
Headwaters State Park, **155**
Hebard, Dr. Grace Raymond, **172**, **176**, **188**
Helena, **xii**, **16**, **47**, **107**, **114**, **115**, **116**, **160**, **179**, **185**, **195**
Hellinger, Dean, **150**
Henneberry, Archie, **43**
Henry Bonnard Bronze Co., **154**
Hilger, David, **i**, **46**, **82**, **108**, **111**, **120**
Hobart, Mrs. Lowell Fletcher, **28**
Hoffman, Charles W., **121**
Hollister, Captain George S., **161**
Holt, Mrs. Clarence, **53**
Huntsman, Mrs. Iverna Lincoln, **29**

Indian Head Mountain, **168**, **175**
Jackson, **176**
Jacobucci, A., **6**
Jennings, Mrs. E.L., **72**
John Taillie, **83**
Johnson, Mrs. F. H., **160**
Johnson, President Andrew, **15**, **16**
Jordan, Rush, **42**
Keith, Mrs. J.M., **134**, **136**
Kobold, Elmer E. "Slim", **95**
Koch, Peter, **121**
Kramlick, Keith, **196**
Kuhr, Mrs. Max, **104**
Lakota Sioux, **115**
LaMotte, Captain R.S., **17**
Lane, Catherine T., **68**
Lang, Miss Anne M., **134**
LaTray, Les, **122**
LaTray, Mose, **120**, **122**
Leavitt, Congressman Scott, **46**, **108**, **160**
Lemhi Pass, **vii**, **ix**, **175**, **187**
Lewistown, **xii**, **113**, **119**, **125**
Liggett, Major General Hunter, **90**
Linn, Mrs. Kate Sturgis Poindexter, **58**
Livingston, **xiii**, **129**
Lockwood, Mrs. Mary S., **182**
Logan, Captain William, **159**, **161**
Logan, Sidney M., **160**
Lolo, **xiii**, **133**

Long, Mrs. E.A., **120**
Love, Mrs. R.V., **xi**, **193**
Luebke, Amelia and John, **126**
Lynn, Miss Leone, **20**
MaGilvra, E.E., **168**
Mailey, August, **169**
Mann Gulch memorial, 109
Mansfield, Senator Mike, **168**
Martin, Mrs. E. Broox, **v**, **16**, **20**, **154**, **176**
May, Mrs. Fred E., **xi**
McClintock, Mike, **2**
McConochie, Mayor Stewart, **120**
McCormack, Lieutenant Governor W.S., **82**
McCormick, Washington J., **46**
McGeorge, Benna Nichols \b, 149
McIlhattan, Mrs. Robert L. (Sharon), **130**
McIntosh, Jack, **170**
McIntyre, Mrs. A.J., **6**
McKee, Robert, **16**
McKinney, Mrs. C.A., **82**
McVey, Mrs. Henry, **194**
Metis, **104**, **120**
Metlen, B. J., **188**
Miles City, **xiii**, **139**, **143**
Miles, General Nelson A., **97**, **99**, **144**
Miller, Mrs. Hugh J. (Georgiana Cole), **182**
Miller, Vicki, **29**

Mitchell, Mayor H.B., **82**
Mondale, Mrs. Walter, **189**
Montana Historical Society, **i**, **25**, **39**, **104**, **111**, **141**, **166**, **186**
Montana Power Company, **82**
Montana State Park, **45**, **81**, **93**, **133**, **165**, **177**
Moore, Mrs. Clinton H., **53**, **154**
Morley, Mrs. E.A., **53**, **155**
Mueller, O.O., **115**
Murray, Mrs. Thomas, **194**
Mylnechuk, Larry, **197**
Nash, Archdeacon, **188**
National Historic Landmark, **9**, **45**, **63**, **68**, **93**, **133**, **189**
National Historic Trail, **97**, **189**
National Register of Historic Places, **23**, **25**, **47**, **95**, **105**, **113**, **119**, **137**, **159**, **162**, **165**, **168**
Nelson, Miss Barbara, **134**
Nelson, Mrs. A.T., **78**
Nelson, Mrs. O.B., **82**
New York State, **192**
Nez Perce, **97**, **99**, **115**, **161**
Nissler, **27**
Northern Pacific Railway, **10**, **11**, **129**, **130**
Northwest Fur Company, **63**, **65**
Northwestern Energy, **27**
Old Forts Trail, **68**, **105**
Olson, Vergie, **150**
Oos, Robin, **150**

Oregon Short Line, **41**, **52**, **53**, **176**

Palmer, Mrs. G.P. (Berniece Metlen), **193**

Peck, Colonel Campbell K., **72**

Pershing, General John J., **105**

Peters, Mrs. Hyram, **72**

Piazzola, JoAnn, **29**, **68**, **78**, **149**

Pickett, Mrs. Frank, **2**

Pickett, Mrs. Frank J. (Bonnie), **155**

Pilon, Mrs. Orrion, **2**, **170**, **184**

Plummer, Henry, **47**, **177**

Poff, Mrs. Roger, **170**

Point of Rocks. *See* Beaverhead Rock

Poole, Mrs. Herbert P., **194**

Pouch, Mrs. William H. (Helena), **58**

Powderville, **139**

Prescott, Mrs. A.K., **186**

Probst, Miss Ethel E., **194**

Rasmusson, Mrs. C.A., **v**, **xi**, **16**, **78**, **94**, **108**, **111**, **186**

Rattle Snake Cliff, **175**

Rattlesnake Cliffs, **58**, **59**, **168**

Reckard, Mrs. H.E., **6**

Redman, John and Mary, **23**

Reed, Alonzo S., **114**, **119**

Renisch, Ella Lydia Arnold, **63**, **66**

Richardson, Dick, **140**

Richardson, T.C., **196**

Rife, Mrs. Ike, **166**

Road Agent Rock, **175**

Rocky Boy's Reservation, **105**

Sacajawea, **10**, **17**, **51**, **108**, **153**, **166**, **167**, **171**, **173**, **187**

Sacajawea Historical Area, **189**

Sacajawea Park, **189**

Salitros, Peggy, **78**

Sarvice Berrie Vallie, **168**, **175**

Scheuber, Mrs., **130**

Schofield, Brian, **114**

Schreiber, Mrs. Virginia Lee (August), **169**

Schwidde, Mrs. Jess T., **126**, **194**

Scott, Laura Tolman, **v**, **x**, **xiii**, **29**, **42**, **58**, **151**, **167**, **172**, **174**, **176**, **177**, **187**, **188**

Scott, Major General Hugh L., **90**

Scott, Mrs. J.W. (Laura Tolman), **53**, **154**

Selway Bridge, **175**

Shelby, **xiii**, **147**

Sheridan, General Phil H., **89**, **90**

Sherman, Mrs. J.G., **6**

Sholey, Diane, **29**

Shoshone, **52**, **53**, **94**, **154**, **156**, **171**, **173**, **187**

Shoshone Cove, **168**, **175**

Simpson, Alva A., **188**

Sioux, **72**, **94**, **103**, **104**

Smith, Miss Louise (later Mrs. Bill Beedie), **126**

Smith, Rev. Edward, **53**
Sons of the American Revolution, **ii, 6, 149, 155, 156**
Spray, Charles, **156**
Spurling, J.E., **11**
Squires, G.R., **176**
**State Historical Society**, **xi**, **82, 108, 120**
Stearns, Hal, **189**
Stevenson, Miss Marjorie, **126, 194**
Stewart, Governor S.V., **160**
Stone, Caroline Reed, **147**
Story, Nelson, **121**
Sullivan, Jere, **66**
Taber, Mrs. Eugene E., **194**
Tallant, Jennie Stilwell, **23, 24, 182, 193**
Teigen, Mons, **126**
Terry, General H., **16, 17**
Tester, Senator Jon, **150**
Thompson, Miss Jean, **20**
Thompson, Mrs. W.T., **20**
Three Forks, **xiii, 153**
Three Thousand Mile Island, **ix, 177**
Tilton, F.L., **191**
Toole, Governor Joseph H., **66**
Toole, K. Ross, **104, 166**
Torkelson, Mrs. Alexander, **72**
Trail Creek, **175**
Tuss, Tony, **126**

Twin Bridges, **165**
Upham, Rear Admiral Frank P., **90**
Van Camps, **176**
Vandegrift, O.T., **43**
Vickers, Robert, **94**
Vinge, Marion, **126**
Virginia City, **38, 47, 58, 175, 179**
Walker, Mrs. William S., **2**
Warn, Mrs. C.C., **186**
Washington D.C., **181**
Washington, Dennis R. and Phyllis, **27**
Washington, Dennis R.-Montana Resources, **27**
Wasson, Mary DeVeny, **192**
Wasson, Mr. R. Gordon, **194**
Wasson, Mrs. Edmund (Mary DeVeny), **24**
Weaver, Anna Beckman, **85**
Wendell Cannon Monument Works, **28**
Wetzel, W.S., **66**
Wheeler, Judy, **150**
Wheeler, Olin D., **53, 130**
Whitcomb, Oliver, **16**
White Bear Island, **178**
White Sulphur Springs, **xiii, 159**
White, John, **46**
Wilbur, R.R., **134**
Wilcox, Ella Wheeler, **183**
Wiley, Mrs. H.L., **72**

Wiley, Mrs. Kay, **176**
Willett, Mrs. G.A., **186**
Woods, Mrs. Frank, **6**
Woodside, Mrs. Elfreda, **47, 170**

Woodside, Mrs. Elfreda (J. Fred), **29, 58, 59, 168, 189**
Yates, Mrs. M.B., **78**
Young, Mrs. Morris, **194**

---

**ABOUT THE AUTHORS**

Janice S. Hand, a 3rd generation DAR member, is chapter regent Silver Bow Chapter, NSDAR and an associate member of the Mount Hyalite Chapter, NSDAR. Cheryl A. Genovese is honorary chapter regent, Mount Hyalite Chapter (signifying she is a former chapter regent). Together, they co-chair the MSSDAR Historic Preservation Committee and wrote this book for you.

www.ingramcontent.com/pod-product-compliance
Lightning Source LLC
Chambersburg PA
CBHW071354290426
44108CB00014B/1547